Building Intercultural Competence for Ministers

MODULES FOR
TRAINING WORKSHOP

In Fulfillment of the Priority Plan of the Bishops of the United States in Recognition of Cultural Diversity

Committee on Cultural Diversity in the Church

UNITED STATES CONFERENCE OF CATHOLIC BISHOPS
WASHINGTON, DC

ISBN 978-1-60137-301-4
First printing, August 2012

A new evangelization is synonymous with mission, requiring the capacity to set out anew, go beyond boundaries and broaden horizons. The new evangelization is the opposite of self-sufficiency, a withdrawal into oneself, a status quo mentality and an idea that pastoral programs are simply to proceed as they did in the past. Today, a "business as usual" attitude can no longer be the case. Some local Churches, already engaged in renewal, reconfirm the fact that now is the time for the Church to call upon every Christian community to evaluate their pastoral practice on the basis of the missionary character of their programs and activities.

Synod of Bishops XIII Ordinary General Assembly
The New Evangelization for the Transmission of the Christian Faith, Lineamenta, no. 10

CONTENTS

MODULE 3: DEVELOP INTERCULTURAL COMMUNICATION SKILLS IN PASTORAL SETTINGS

INTRODUCTION

In 2007, the United States Conference of Catholic Bishops (USCCB) established several priorities for action during the 2008-11 planning cycle. One of those priorities was "recognition of cultural diversity." In highlighting this priority, the bishops were not only pointing to the profound demographic transformation that has been taking place in the United States and in the Church over several decades, they were also manifesting the Catholic Church's concern with diversity not just as a practical matter but as something integral to the Church's very identity and mission.

The focus on cultural diversity is grounded on the urgent need to grow in knowledge and develop appropriate attitudes and skills for the purpose of carrying out the Church's mission of evangelization. One cannot adequately preach, teach, or form persons in the Catholic faith without attending to the ways in which Catholic faith and identity become embodied in culture. Proficiency in matters of culture and intercultural relations is an essential feature of the ongoing process of conversion by which the Gospel becomes life for people. The New Evangelization, so ardently championed by Pope Benedict XVI and his predecessors, hinges on the acquisition of competencies that advance both the proclamation of the Gospel and the intercultural dialogue leading to the Christian conversion of individuals and entire cultures.

The program outlined in this manual is aimed at anyone involved in ecclesial ministry. This, of course, includes bishops, priests, and deacons; religious men and women; and lay ecclesial ministers who serve in dioceses, parishes, schools, and Catholic organizations.

The background and proficiency offered by this program are for every cultural, ethnic, or racial group in the Church. While it is true that persons of European ancestry constitute the majority of those involved in ecclesial ministries today, very sizable cohorts of Catholics from all cultural families enjoy positions of leadership, not only among their own groups but increasingly among diverse communities. The reality of shared or multicultural parishes is becoming the norm in many places.

Building Intercultural Competence for Ministers (BICM) should therefore be offered to persons from all the major cultural families, not just European Americans, for example. At the Cultural Diversity Network Convocation held at the University of Notre Dame in May 2010, the participants were selected from among six major families: (1) European Americans; (2) Hispanics/Latinos; (3) African Americans; (4) Asian and Pacific Islanders; (5) Native Americans; and (6) migrants, refugees, and travelers. These categories reflect the subcommittees the bishops have established for the Committee on Cultural Diversity.

What is particularly notable about identifying these categories is the fact that they may be used to establish certain equality among all the groups, whatever their histories and relative numbers in relation to the entire Catholic (diocesan or parish) population. In this approach, the European American context—the prevailing or dominant culture—is not presumed to provide the only, or even the main, framework or paradigm for the other communities.

This helps create a "level playing field" and facilitates the development of greater trust and mutuality among all groups, including the European Americans. It is recommended that groups seeking to apply the methods for building intercultural relations and communications contained in these modules consider adopting this same approach.

One of the important, if not essential, lessons learned in the process of convening diverse groups at Notre Dame was the central role that storytelling played in setting the tone for everything that followed. Each community was eager to share its stories, and everyone found them engaging and informative. While a simple procedure, this was the key to beginning the delicate process of intercultural encounter in an inclusive, effective way. As such, creating opportunities for meaningful storytelling is essential in dioceses, parishes, and organizations that seek to build greater Christian community among diverse cultural families.

Using These Guidelines: A Practical Overview

The following pages provide five modules designed to assist those leading workshops on building intercultural competence for ministers. The intent is to offer ministry leaders an opportunity to achieve a basic level of awareness and proficiency in the area of intercultural competency through the five guidelines recommended by the USCCB Committee on Cultural Diversity in the Church.

STRUCTURE OF THESE GUIDELINES

These guidelines are divided into five sections representing five different modules:

Module 1: Frame issues of diversity theologically in terms of the Church's identity and mission to evangelize.
Module 2: Seek an understanding of culture and how it works.
Module 3: Develop intercultural communication skills in pastoral settings.
Module 4: Expand one's knowledge of the obstacles which impede effective intercultural relations.
Module 5: Foster ecclesial integration rather than assimilation in Church settings with a spirituality of hospitality, reconciliation, and mission.

The appendices have additional resources such as a glossary of terms, supplementary resources, and sample introductory and concluding prayer services to support the application of the competencies outlined in this guide.

HOW TO USE THE BUILDING INTERCULTURAL COMPETENCE FOR MINISTERS (BICM) GUIDELINES

At the beginning of each module is a list of goals and outcomes clearly identified to guide the training process. There are also group activities specific to each module that encourage effective interaction and constructive group dynamics. This promotes an atmosphere that is most conducive to open authentic dialogue within a group setting.

Additionally, each section features a list of resources relevant to that specific module. The glossary of terms at the end of this resource provides useful terminology in the area of cultural diversity.

ADDITIONAL RESOURCES

It is recommended that further reading be done on this topic, such as the material outlined in the *Catholic Cultural Diversity Network Convocation Notebook*, which is a valuable additional resource based on the experience of the Catholic Cultural Diversity Network Convocation (CCDNC). For instance, the process by which "witnesses" were selected to voice the stories of their particular community is detailed in the *Notebook* available on the USCCB Cultural Diversity in the Church web page.

The BICM video gives an introductory overview of the workshops and the overall vision that brought forth the development of the competencies. It serves as an inspirational visual guide on the work that has been piloted by the Committee on Cultural Diversity in the Church.

Finally, the results of a *National Consultation on Best Practices in Culturally Diverse/Shared Parishes* will also be available soon on the USCCB website and in print.

Additional resources on this topic and updates on workshops and related events can also be found on the USCCB website. Search for "intercultural competencies" or go to *www.usccb.org/about/cultural-diversity-in-the-church/ intercultural-competencies.*

FOREWORD

"Go, therefore, and make disciples of all nations . . . teaching them to observe all that I have commanded you."

—Matthew 28:19-20

The Catholic bishops of the United States, in their priority plan entitled "Deepen Faith, Nurture Hope, Celebrate Life," chose recognition of cultural diversity with emphasis on Hispanic ministry as one of five priorities for the planning cycle of 2008-11. In response to this priority, several activities emerged as recommended by the Task Force on Cultural Diversity, which was established by the USCCB Committee on Priorities and Plans in 2008 and is chaired by Bishop Ricardo Ramírez, CSB. The foundational activity proposed by the task force and endorsed by the full body of bishops was the development of guidelines for intercultural competence. This course has been designed to express these guidelines in the form of competencies. To disseminate this resource as widely as possible, regional workshops are being planned. A core group of trainers will be recruited and trained in providing pastoral leaders of all cultural backgrounds with this introductory course. What follows here is additional information about the content, some of the adult learning methodology, and other resources.

In light of demographic changes taking place throughout the nation today, these competencies are increasingly necessary for effective pastoral leadership in the Catholic Church in the United States. Although traditional pastoral approaches, such as the personal or national parish, have been useful over the years, they are increasingly more difficult to sustain or inadequate for the growing diversity of the Church. Today's urban and suburban parishes are becoming "shared" or multicultural parishes. They find themselves serving a daunting combination of nationalities, language groups, cultures, and races, going well beyond the monolingual and monocultural approaches of either the national parish or the assimilated suburban parish of just a few decades ago.

More importantly, knowledge, attitudes, and skills in intercultural and interracial relations are indispensable requirements for engaging in the Church's evangelizing mission to preach, teach, and witness to the Gospel. To evangelize is to engage cultures and transform them in light of the Gospel of Jesus Christ (see *Evangelii Nuntiandi*, no. 20). Pope Benedict XVI, recalling us to the vision of a New Evangelization first proposed by Pope John Paul II, has given renewed urgency to the task of engaging culture and "re-proposing" belief in Christ and his Gospel in the context of a secularized world (Pope Benedict XVI, Homily, Solemnity of SS. Peter and Paul, June 28, 2010).

The course draws on the knowledge and practices derived from cultural anthropology as well as the insights of intercultural studies. At the same time, it is grounded in the Church's teaching about the human person and Christian spirituality. This course will frame many of the questions about the cultural plurality of American society within the larger context of the Church's identity and mission to engage cultures for the sake of the Gospel and evangelize them.

The workshop is directed to all those engaged in some form of ecclesial ministry, including bishops, priests, deacons, religious men and women, lay ecclesial ministers, and other pastoral agents. It brings participants to an introductory level of familiarity with intercultural relations for ministry, providing both theological and spiritual foundations. The members of the Committee on Cultural Diversity in the Church hope the knowledge, attitudes, and skills proposed here will become common competencies for all ministers in the United States.

May the intercession of our Blessed Mother, Santa María de Guadalupe, grace this earnest pastoral effort with the wisdom and grace of her Son, Jesus.

✠ Jaime Soto
Chair, Committee on Cultural Diversity in the Church
United States Conference of Catholic Bishops
September 15, 2011

MODULE 1

Frame Issues of Diversity Theologically in Terms of the Church's Identity and Mission to Evangelize

GOALS

1. To better understand the meaning and purpose of both evangelization and the New Evangelization
2. To examine the U.S. prevailing culture in light of the New Evangelization
3. To explore key ethnic and cultural groups in the Church as well as the opportunities and challenges these present for the New Evangelization
4. To understand the meaning of inculturation, or evangelization of cultures

OUTCOMES

- Ability to articulate an understanding of the Church's mission and identity in terms of evangelization and its relation to the New Evangelization
- Familiarity with the basic elements of evangelization in terms of "four pillars" and examples of how evangelization engages individuals and cultures in today's world
- A grasp of the theological foundations for the Church's mission to evangelize in Scripture, tradition, and contemporary Church teaching

This module places the entire course within the framework of the Church's identity and mission to evangelize and the New Evangelization. Pope John Paul II first used the term "New Evangelization" in his encyclical *Redemptoris Missio*. It is to be understood as presenting anew or, as Pope Benedict XVI has put it, "re-proposing" the faith of Jesus Christ, especially in places where adherence to the Gospel has already taken root but is now in decline, so that believers may grow more deeply in discipleship. Pope John Paul II added his own insight about the process of evangelization and spoke of the New Evangelization as proclaiming the Gospel with new methods, expressions, and ardor.

The task begins by examining the New Evangelization as it might apply to the United States—especially to its prevailing culture—and then focuses on the essential need to develop greater capacity for intercultural communication. In so doing, we may see new challenges and opportunities for presenting the message of Jesus Christ. The module refers to the Catholic bishops of the United States' document *Go and Make Disciples* as expressing their vision of evangelization in providing the framework for the Church's identity and mission in the United States.

What Is Evangelization?

The purpose of the Church is to evangelize: "The Church has received from the apostles Christ's solemn command to proclaim the truth which saves, and it must carry it to the very ends of the earth" (*Lumen Gentium*, no. 17). To *evangelize* means literally to "spread the Good News." At the heart of that message is the encounter with Jesus Christ and the salvation he brings to the world. From that encounter comes incorporation into the Body of Christ, which is the Church. The Church's very nature is missionary—that is, to share this message with the entire world. Thus, missionary activity is not something left solely to the professional foreign missionary; it is a responsibility incumbent on all believers.

In his 1975 apostolic exhortation *Evangelii Nuntiandi*, Pope Paul VI elaborated profoundly on the meaning of evangelization. It is not directed only to the salvation of individual souls, but to entire societies and cultures. In his understanding of the "evangelization of cultures," those values and patterns of living that shape individual lives and societies are brought into encounter with Christ so that all may have life in abundance (see Jn 10:10). Evangelization can be understood as having four pillars:

1. Conversion: a personal encounter with Jesus Christ
2. The evangelization of cultures: the encounter between a people's rituals, symbols, and myths (narratives) and the Gospel, leading to the transformation of culture (inculturation)
3. Liberation: the transformation of social, economic, and political orders in light of gospel values of life and human dignity
4. Ecumenical and interreligious dialogue: work to bring about the unity of all peoples in pursuit of Jesus' mandate

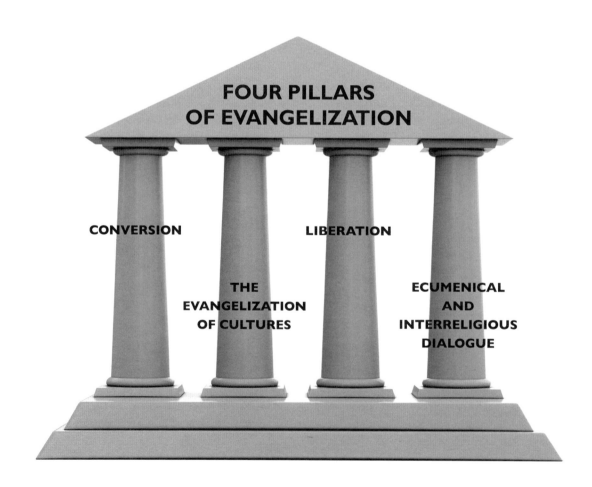

FOUR PILLARS OF EVANGELIZATION

CONVERSION

THE EVANGELIZATION OF CULTURES

LIBERATION

ECUMENICAL AND INTERRELIGIOUS DIALOGUE

In *Redemptoris Missio*, Pope John Paul II focused on re-igniting the fire of faith in the baptized so that they might be evangelizers of those around them. He urged the faithful to seek out the new *areopagoi*—that is, the new social forums in which the faith is to be presented. Indeed, the call to a New Evangelization became a cornerstone of John Paul II's papacy.

Pope Benedict XVI has continued the call for a New Evangelization. His homily to the Catholic bishops of the United States in April 2008 in Washington, D.C., underscored the importance of the New Evangelization for America. In July 2010, he established a Pontifical Council for the New Evangelization. He has reminded the faithful of the function of the Court of the Gentiles, which brought non-Jews into dialogue with people from all cultures in the precincts of the Temple in Jerusalem.

In *Go and Make Disciples*, the Catholic bishops of the United States stress outreach in dialogue based on a clear sense of Catholic identity. They outline three goals in this document: (1) to deepen the faith of Catholics so that they might share their faith with others, (2) to invite all in the United States to hear the message of salvation, and (3) to foster gospel values in society.

What Are the Challenges of the New Evangelization in the United States?

The ongoing Pew Forum on Religion and Public Life (*www.pewforum.org*) and reports from the Center for Applied Research in the Apostolate (CARA) at Georgetown University (*cara.georgetown.edu*) provide rich background material for understanding the religious and demographic context as well as the challenges facing the Catholic Church in the United States. Much of what follows here is culled from these sources.

The United States is the fifth most multicultural country in the world (after Australia, Switzerland, Canada, and Sweden, though these countries have much smaller populations) (see Organization for Economic Cooperation and Development, *International Migration Outlook Annual Report*, 2006 Edition [OECD Publishing, 2006]). It has also been a land of immigration. The presence of so many cultures has given the nation a pluralist quality.

Although Catholics make up the single largest religious body in the United States (some 24 percent of the population), the prevailing culture has a Protestant flavor. Indeed, anti-Catholicism has marked much of U.S. history.

The United States is a *secularized* society, as are most financially well-off countries around the world today. However, it is not as secularized as many countries in Europe or as Canada, Australia, and New Zealand. Fifty-eight percent of Americans say they pray at least once a day (see *religions.pewforum.org/comparisons*). Nevertheless, the number of Americans who claim to have no religious belief at all continues to rise (see Barry A. Kosmin and Ariela Keysar, *American Religious Identification Survey* [ARIS 2008] *Summary Report* [Hartford, CT: Institute for the Study of Secularism in Society and Culture, 2009], and Keyser, Egon Mayer, and Kosmin, "No Religion: A Profile of America's Unchurched," *Public Perspective* 14[1]: 28-32).

Although the Catholic Church has continued to grow in numbers (something not experienced by the so-called "mainline" Protestant churches), this growth has been largely because of immigration and immigrants' larger families (see Robert D. Putnam and David E. Campbell, *American Grace* [New York: Simon and Schuster, 2010], 138). Many Catholics drift away from the Church, especially as young adults. It has been said that if all the former Catholics in the United States were to constitute a church denomination, it would perhaps be the second largest church in the country, after the Catholic Church (2007 U.S. Religious Landscape Survey, Pew Forum on Religion and Public Life).

Individualism has long been a characteristic of the prevailing culture in the United States. Connected with that individualism is a strong sense of freedom to choose one's lifestyle and profession. Individualism can make space for creativity and achievement, but it can also be a source of selfishness.

Because of its wealth, U.S. society can be a *materialistic* one, meaning that having more and more possessions becomes the criterion for self-fulfillment and success. Recent studies have indicated that while the United States is one of the richest countries in the world, it ranks only about fourteenth in terms of happiness (see *www.nationmaster.com/graph/lif_hap_lev_qui_hap-lifestyle-happiness-level-quite-happy*).

Where do Catholics find themselves regarding secularism, individualism, and materialism? Secularism traditionally carries with it important values such as respect for human rights and freedom of religion. When the secular crowds out the religious, however, it needs to be challenged. Religion provides important pathways to the transcendent that every society needs.

Respect for the dignity of every human person is a central tenet of Christian faith. In Catholic social teaching, the basic social unit is not the individual, but the family. Catholic faith sees every human being as interdependent with a community, not as solitary individuals.

Material goods are necessary for human survival and well-being, but when material goods become idols—taking away our relation to God and putting something else in its place—the quest for material goods needs to be critiqued.

The New Evangelization in a Society and Church of Many Cultures

So what does the New Evangelization look like in light of a culturally pluralistic society and Church? Here are some thoughts for reflection:

- The faith of Native Americans, African Americans, and immigrants from elsewhere may serve as a stimulus to the faith and devotion of those in the Church who are more aligned with the prevailing culture. Devotion to family among immigrant populations may bring about a rethinking of how the family structure has eroded in a secularized and globalized society.
- A fresh or a first encounter with Jesus Christ, seen through the eyes of those marginalized by the prevailing culture, can rekindle commitment to social justice and *solidarity*.
- The response to evangelization is *conversion*, a recommitment to Jesus Christ and his message of salvation. As people from different cultures encounter one another, they may be able to see their faith in a new light.
- The Catholic Church is the most ethnically diverse of all the U.S. denominations (see Putnam and Campbell, op. cit., 292). If we, as Catholics, can

find ways of creating genuine *communion* among the various groups within the Church, we can serve as a model for the rest of society.

- Although first-generation immigrants often experience an increase in religiosity upon coming to the United States (partly because their faith is a form of continuity with their lives in their homelands), there is significant falloff in the second generation (see Paul Perl, Jennifer Z. Greely, and Mark M. Gray, "How Many Hispanics Are Catholic? A Review of Survey Data" [Washington, DC: CARA, 2004]). What forms should the New Evangelization take in young adult ministry?

A Theology for Intercultural Ministry

A theology for intercultural ministry finds its sources in the Christian understanding of the human person and in a theology of the Church as communion, as truly "catholic" (or universal), and as missionary in nature.

Christian Anthropology: The Understanding of the Human Person

Christianity bases its understanding of the human person on the first Creation story in Genesis. There we read that human beings are made in the "image" and "likeness" of God (Gn 1:26-27). The dignity of human beings is rooted in their creation in this image and likeness of God, and "it shines forth in the communion of persons, in the likeness of the unity of the divine persons among themselves" (CCC, no. 1702). It is in this light that Christians understand that every person, regardless of race or ethnicity, is to be treated with dignity and respect.

The Church as Communion

The Church is a communion modeled on the love among Father, Son, and Holy Spirit. It seeks to mirror that communion of Divine Persons in the way it welcomes and gathers in all peoples—"every tribe and tongue, people and nation" (Rev 5:9). As Pope John Paul II put it in *Novo Millennio Ineunte*, the Church is to be the "home and school of communion" (no. 43). The Church is not sectarian and meant only for a chosen few.

The Church as Catholic

Moreover, our Church is a *catholic* Church; in its universality, it intends to gather in all peoples without exception. It is a communion in diversity, not in uniformity. It is Catholic, too, in its believing all that the Lord has revealed. It is within this frame of mind that the Church undertakes ministry among all cultures for the sake of bringing all people together into communion with one Lord and one common Father.

The Church as Mission

From Vatican II to *Evangelii Nuntiandi* and *Redemptoris Missio*, recent Church teaching has stressed the missionary identity of the Church. Both Pope John Paul II and Pope Benedict XVI have referred to the Church as being missionary in its entirety. By virtue of Baptism, all are called to be missionary disciples of the Lord Jesus Christ. The Fifth Conference of the Bishops of Latin America and the Caribbean extensively developed the theme of missionary discipleship in the 2007 *Concluding Document* of Aparecida. One of the implications of the Church's missionary character is precisely the central role of intercultural knowledge, skills, and attitudes that enable ministers of the Gospel to proclaim Christ's message effectively among all nations.

RESOURCES

Dulles, Cardinal Avery, SJ. *The Catholicity of the Church*. Oxford: Clarendon Press, 1985.

Fernández, Eduardo, SJ, Kenneth McGuire, CSP, and Anne Hansen. *Culture-Sensitive Ministry: Helpful Strategies for Pastoral Ministers*, NY: Paulist Press, 2010.

Lucido, Frank (ed.). *Reflections on Inculturation*. Washington, DC: National Catholic Educational Association, 2002.

Pope John Paul II. *Redemptoris Missio (On the Permanent Validity of the Church's Missionary Mandate)*. Washington, DC: USCCB, 1991.

Pope Paul VI. *Evangelii Nuntiandi (On Evangelization in the Modern World)*. Washington, DC: USCCB, 1975.

Wuerl, Cardinal Donald W. *Disciples of the Lord Sharing the Vision: A Pastoral Letter on the New Evangelization*. Washington, DC: Archdiocese of Washington, 2010.

GROUP ACTIVITIES

1. Small group exercise based on biblical readings regarding faith and culture: Genesis 11:1-9, Matthew 15:21-28, John 4:5-42, Acts of the Apostles 10:1-35, Acts of the Apostles 15:1-33, and Galatians 2: 11-16.

2. Small group discussions regarding the following topics and how they relate to Catholic identity and values: (a) the prevailing culture in the United States; (b) particular non-European cultures (such as Hispanic/Latino, Asian Pacific Islander, Haitian, etc.); (c) migrants, refugees, and travelers; and (d) youth and young adult cultures.

MODULE 2

Seek an Understanding of Culture and How It Works

GOALS

1. To familiarize participants with the basic concepts that underlie intercultural competence: concepts of culture; dimensions of interculturality (knowledge, skills, and attitudes); and different indices for understanding culture
2. To develop the communication skills needed to function in different kinds of cultures

OUTCOMES

- Define culture and identify ways in which culture influences communication.
- Understand how cultures differ beneath the surface and how cultures respond differently to similar situations.
- Create a framework of ideas that can be applied to understanding the major concepts of intercultural communication.

This module introduces participants to basic categories used to facilitate intercultural understanding and communication.

Culture and Intercultural Competence

What Is Culture?

There is no agreed upon definition of culture. But we quickly see cultural differences. A working definition would suggest that culture has three distinct dimensions:

1. *Cultures have ideas and ways of expressing them.* Cultures have *beliefs* about God, themselves, and others. Cultures carry *values* that shape their ways of living and interacting with others. Cultures have a *language* that conveys their ideas, feelings, and ways of living.
2. *Cultures have behaviors.* Cultures have rules about what is proper and improper behavior. Roles—for example, within the family—have distinctive features. They have ways of celebrating and extending hospitality.
3. *Cultures have material dimensions.* Cultures have material, outward signs that express and reflect their ideas and beliefs. Cultures have their special foods (what is eaten every day and what is eaten on special occasions). Among other things, they also have unique modes of dressing and furnishing their homes.

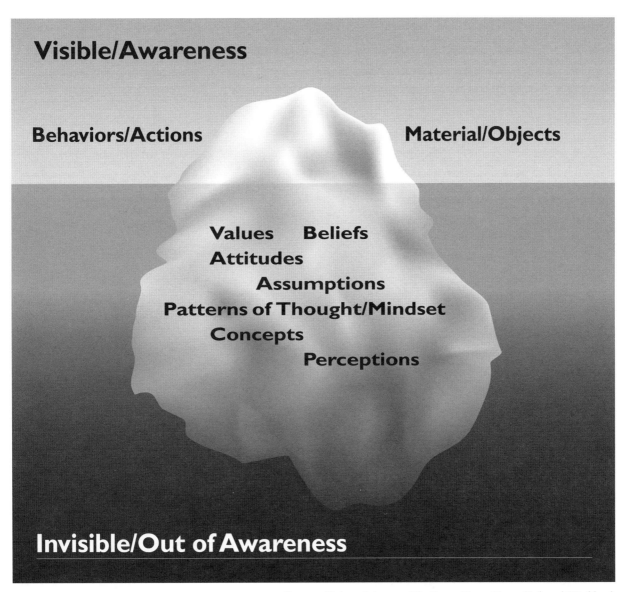

Visible/Awareness

Behaviors/Actions   Material/Objects

Values   Beliefs
Attitudes
Assumptions
Patterns of Thought/Mindset
Concepts
Perceptions

Invisible/Out of Awareness

Source: Culture Matters: The Peace Corps Cross-Cultural Workbook

Culture has been likened to an iceberg. Just as an iceberg has parts above the waterline, a larger, invisible part remains underwater. Culture, too, has some aspects that are observable and others that can only be suspected, imagined, or intuited. Also like an iceberg, that part of culture that is visible (observable) is only a small part of a much larger whole.

Some descriptions of culture:

The word "culture" comes from the Latin verb *colere*, which means to cultivate the ground. Eventually, the expression *cultura animi*, the culture of souls, came to designate the personal formative process of the individual. When the process of personal formation is understood in intellectual terms, a "cultured person" is someone who simply knows a lot. However, personal formation is a process with intellectual, affective, ethical, and practical components. It touches on everything that is characteristically human. Culture is what shapes the human being as specifically human.

—USCCB, *The Hispanic Presence in the New Evangelization in the United States* (1996), 17

Culture primarily expresses how people live and perceive the world, one another, and God. Culture is the set of values by which a people judge, accept, and live what is considered important within the community.

—USCCB, *National Pastoral Plan for Hispanic Ministry* (1988), 69

Culture is the particular way in which a human group interprets life and relates with nature, God, the world, and other peoples. Culture is not accidental, but an integral part of human life. Culture is lived and expressed through traditions, language, relationships, food and music, and religious expressions. It embraces the totality of life of the group and the life of each individual who belongs to it; therefore, all human beings relate and respond to God and express this faith from and within their culture.

—USCCB, "Principles of Inculturation of the Catechism of the Catholic Church," *The Living Light* 31 (1994)

The word "culture" in its general sense indicates all those factors by which man refines and unfolds his manifold spiritual and bodily qualities. It means his effort to bring the world itself under his control by his knowledge and his labor. It includes the fact that by improving customs and institutions he renders social life more human both within the family and the civic community. Finally, it is a feature of culture that throughout the course of time man expresses, communicates, and conserves in his works great spiritual experiences and desires, so that these may be of advantage to the progress of many, even of the whole human family.

—*Gaudium et Spes*, no. 53, "The Proper Development of Culture"

Ways People Talk About Culture

There are three major ways people talk about culture. They are often referred to as *classical*, *modern*, and *postmodern*.

- **Classical.** Culture in this sense means the highest artistic products of a people: its poetry, its literature, its music, and its artwork. In this sense, some people are "cultured," and others are not. So, if you go to the opera on Saturday night, some people would say you have culture. If you go bowling, some people may think you lack culture. Culture has a normative sense here.
- **Modern.** Culture in this sense means the unity of language, custom, and territory. Thus, if a people share a common language, have similar customs and material objects, and live within a defined territory, they represent a culture. In this sense, everyone has a culture—you are Mexican, Filipino, African American, etc. Cultures can be seen in smaller units as well: different regions of Mexico, the Philippines, etc. This is the understanding of culture that shapes most of our talk about multicultural or intercultural realities.
- **Postmodern.** Especially in urban settings where cultures (in the modern sense just discussed) rub up against one another, people may be speaking their traditional language as well as another language. They may adapt customs of their neighbors. And they don't have their own defined territory. The place in which they find themselves is really a forum where things are borrowed and crafted together to create a way of life. This is what is known as postmodern culture. It is especially prevalent among second- and third-generation immigrants and youth.

In Church documents, both classical and modern senses of culture are used. The late Pope John Paul II, in his visits to many countries, would give two speeches on culture. The first would be to the "culture-makers": artists, journalists, and intellectuals. This is an example of the classical understanding of culture. Then he would give a speech to a beleaguered minority group, urging them to hold on to their culture. This is an example of the modern sense of culture.

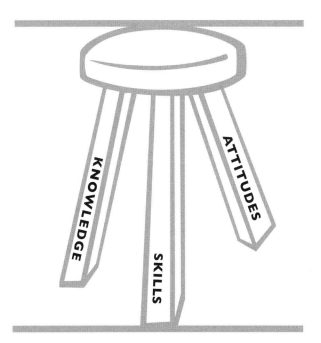

What Is Intercultural Competence?

Intercultural competence is the capacity to communicate, relate, and work across cultural boundaries. It involves developing capacity in three areas: *knowledge*, *skills*, and *attitudes*.

Knowledge involves the following:

- Knowledge of more than one perspective on things
- Knowledge of different interpretations of the same cultural reality
- Knowledge of general dynamics of intercultural communication
- Knowledge of more than one's first language

Skills entail the following:

- Ability to empathize
- Ability to tolerate ambiguity
- Ability to adapt communication and behavior

Attitudes include the following:

- Openness to others and other cultures
- Wanting to learn and engage other cultures
- Understanding intercultural interaction as a way of life, not a problem to be solved
- Mindfulness

These areas of knowledge, skills, and attitudes function in two different ways, depending on whether you are part of the prevailing culture or come from another culture:

1. If you are a member of the prevailing culture, you can get along to a great degree with very little knowledge of other cultures, because members of the prevailing culture expect those of other cultures to learn to operate in the prevailing culture. For prevailing-culture people to gain intercultural competence, they may have to learn to think in cultural categories before they can begin to exercise greater competency in moving across cultures.

2. If you are a member of a culture other than the prevailing one, you have already learned a considerable amount about intercultural communication, because you have had to in order to survive in the prevailing culture. You probably already have a grasp of cultural categories at least implicitly—that is, you know how to work with them even if you do not have a name for them. You may have developed what African American philosopher W.E.B. DuBois called a "double consciousness" (from the chapter "Of Our Spiritual Strivings" in his book *The Souls of Black Folk*), meaning you can think in your own distinctive cultural way, and you have found a way to negotiate through a prevailing culture that looks down on you as inferior. You also may carry wounds of being discriminated against, excluded, and treated as less than you really are.

People in ministry need to be able to understand both of these intercultural reactions.

Parameters of Interacting with Other Cultures

Students of intercultural communication suggest that there are some basic parameters or coordinates along which important dimensions of cultural ideas and behaviors can be plotted. We are going to consider five such parameters here. Each of these parameters, presented as "a versus b," should be read like a spectrum. No culture is exclusively one or the other, though every culture will tend to be closer to one end of the spectrum than the other.

The information presented here is adapted especially from the work of Geert Hofstede, a sociologist who studied these dynamics in more than fifty countries around the world, as reported in his book *Culture's Consequences* (2001).

Parameter 1: Collectivism Versus Individualism

This is the most fundamental and important parameter for understanding cultures. It has to do with how we think about groups as a whole and individuals within groups—and whether the group or the individual has priority in our thinking, our values, and our behavior.

Collectivism

In a predominantly collectivist culture, maintaining the group has priority over the individual's hopes and desires. The individual is defined by his or her position in the group: as older or younger, as male or female, as married or unmarried. The group or the elders may make major life decisions, such as about a professional occupation or about a marriage partner, for individuals within the group. Family is understood as the extended family. Maintaining the honor or the "face" of the group is of paramount importance. Loyalty to the group is the highest value. Maintaining harmony within the group is a major concern.

Individualism

In a predominantly individualist culture, the individual has priority over the group. The individual is ultimately responsible for his or her life decisions. The group is, when all is said and done, the sum of the individuals who make up the group. Family is generally understood as the immediate or nuclear family. Loyalty to the larger group is contingent on the group's performance and support of the individual's life. Individuals are expected to be independent and creative, and they are encouraged to seek self-fulfillment. How the individual stands out from the group is an important measure of this.

Further Reflections

Individualism is strongest in Western societies, and it is predominant in about one-third of the world's cultures. Collectivism is more common in East and South Asian societies (especially where Confucian values shape the society) as well as in Latin American and African societies. Collectivism predominates in about two-thirds of the world's cultures. Collectivism is often stronger in rural settings than in urban areas because modernization usually promotes more individualist values. The prevailing culture in the United States is markedly individualist.

Catholic teaching has leaned more toward the collectivist understanding. For example, most would agree that in Catholic social teaching, the basic unit of society is the family, not the individual. At the same time, the dignity of each human person is also a hallmark of Catholic teaching and thought.

Parameter 2: Hierarchy Versus Equality

This parameter charts how power and status are distributed in a group: whether it is highly stratified or whether loci of power are diffuse and unclear. In the literature, this is sometimes called "high power distance versus low power distance."

Hierarchy

Power is unevenly distributed, and inequality is presumed. The more power one has, so also the higher status. Authority is inherited. Sanctions and rewards are based on one's social position. Everyone in the society knows his or her place in the hierarchy. Communication between those who are lower on the power scale and those who are higher is often indirect in nature or carried out by mediators. Because so much communication is indirect, such situations are often termed "high context cultures."

Equality

The power in the group is diffuse and sometimes hard to locate. Locating power is often difficult because of the ideal of equality, but there are often unspoken rules that govern things. Authority is earned. Sanctions and rewards are based on one's performance. People can gain or lose status. Status is often seen as something earned rather than as something ascribed because of one's position. Communication is more direct in this situation. Because communication is more direct, these are often called "low context cultures."

Further Reflections

Collectivist societies usually exhibit some measure of hierarchy; sometimes they exhibit a considerable level of hierarchy. Because communication up the hierarchical scale is indirect, there are many implicit rules to learn for those coming from other cultures. One of the most difficult for outsiders is learning to read when "yes" means "yes" and when "yes" means "no": one does not dishonor one's superiors by saying "no" to them. Egalitarian societies are never completely egalitarian, but they like to present themselves as such. This can make them hard to read for outsiders.

The Catholic Church has strong hierarchical patterns, which often lead to clashes in individualist, more egalitarian societies. Thus, prevailing-culture Americans tend to understand the Church as "People of God" in a much more egalitarian form than it has been understood elsewhere. Catholics coming from more hierarchical societies will often be puzzled by the polarities in the Catholic Church in the United States, where people from a highly individualist setting challenge rules about hierarchical structures and decision making in the Church.

Parameter 3: Low Tolerance of Ambiguity Versus High Tolerance of Ambiguity

This parameter charts the relative importance of rules and degree of causality (what needs to be explained and what does not need to be explained) in a society. In other words, how much ambiguity or uncertainty is allowed in a society? In intercultural communication, some call this parameter "uncertainty avoidance."

Low Tolerance

In cultures with a low tolerance of ambiguity, every event (especially unfortunate ones) needs an explanation. For example, if a young person dies in an accident, God is punishing someone. Rules for behavior are explicit and leave little room for interpretation or for exceptions. People in such cultures work hard to avoid any uncertainty in their worldview.

High Tolerance

There are fewer explicit rules, and those rules can be interpreted in a generous way. A cause does not need to be assigned to every single thing that happens. People in such cultures live with a good deal of ambiguity.

Further Reflections

Rural communities and small-scale cultures tend to be low-tolerance ones. Catholics, especially in majority-Catholic countries, typically were low-tolerance, but that sometimes changes in urban populations. Urbanized populations, which must deal with a great deal of pluralism, tend to be more highly tolerant of ambiguity. Pope Benedict XVI's remarks about the "dictatorship of relativism" are targeted at high-tolerance societies (Joseph Ratzinger, Homily, April 18, 2005). Part of the polarization experienced in the Catholic Church in the United States is between attitudes of low-tolerance and high-tolerance.

Parameter 4: A Masculine Versus a Feminine Understanding of Gender Roles

Geert Hofstede and other researchers talk about "masculinity" versus "femininity" in cultures. By this, they mean how relatively clear and distinct gender roles are intended to be.

"Masculine" Cultures

Gender roles are distinct and clearly allocated. Men are in charge in the public sphere, make decisions, and protect women. They are expected to be achievers and providers for their families. Women are kept in the private or home sphere, where they care for the children and the elderly. In these cultures, women are expected to be nurturing.

"Feminine" Cultures

Gender roles are not clearly defined and tend to overlap. Women and men have an equal role in the public sphere, and they often share responsibility for the care of the household and the children. Decisions are made mutually.

Further Reflections

Western modernity and postmodernity emphasize a more "feminine" approach to gender roles, especially in urban settings. This often clashes with more "masculine" differentiations in rural settings and more "traditional" cultures. Catholic Church documents at the level of the Vatican affirm the equal dignity of women and men, but they tend toward a "masculine" reading of gender roles. The very use of the term "gender" is considered in some circles as a "radical feminist" approach. How to read gender roles is a matter of great contention in Church settings.

Parameter 5: Lived-Experience Versus Abstract Time Orientation

This is a complex area, covering the meaning of time in different communities, how it affects interaction, and what values are privileged in differing understandings of time.

Lived-Experience and Short-Term Approaches to Time

In this approach, time is subjugated to the needs of the community and fostering relationships in the community. Emphasis is on the past and present. Upholding traditions and fulfilling social obligations have priority over thinking about the future.

Thus, a meeting never begins in such cultures until everyone has arrived and each person has had the chance to greet everyone else and inquire about their families. These past relationships determine the present. Long-term planning is not a priority. In these cultures, one typically thinks about the short term and places an emphasis on maintaining human relationships.

Abstract and Long-Term Approaches to Time

Time is a value in itself ("time is money"), and social interactions are to be ordered to its requirements and demands. Meetings focus on the tasks to be accomplished more than the enhancement of human relationships. While emphasis is on the present, such cultures especially concentrate on the future. Abstract ideas and long-term goals are valued, and their achievement is calculated and calibrated into units of time. Human relationships support these possibilities but are secondary.

Thus, meetings begin and end within a certain time segment, and what needs to be done is tailored to fit within that segment. Emphasis is on the achievement of objectives.

Further Reflections

Lived-experience time works best in rural areas, where the rhythms of planting, cultivation, and harvest set the tone for human relationships. Abstract approaches to time have been influenced by industrialization in that tasks are broken down into units and complex organizations determine the role of individual workers within the design. The strength of this approach is its ability to take complex tasks and make them manageable by reducing them to discrete parts or processes.

 # RESOURCES

Arbuckle, Gerald A., SM. *Earthing the Gospel: An Inculturation Handbook for the Pastoral Worker.* Maryknoll, NY: Orbis Books, 1990.

Catechism of the Catholic Church (2nd ed.). Washington, DC: Libreria Editrice Vaticana–USCCB, 2000.

Gallagher, Michael, SJ. *Clashing Symbols: An Introduction to Faith and Culture.* New York: Paulist Press, 1998.

Hofstede, Geert. *Culture's Consequences: Comparing Values, Behaviors, Institutions, and Organizations Across Nations.* Thousand Oaks, CA: Sage Publications, 2001.

Pusch, Margaret D. *Multicultural Education: A Cross-Cultural Training Approach.* New York: Intercultural Press, 1979.

Second Vatican Council. *Pastoral Constitution on the Church in the Modern World* (*Gaudium et Spes*), no. 53. In *The Documents of Vatican II*, edited by Walter M. Abbott. New York: Guild Press, 1996.

WAYS PEOPLE TALK ABOUT CULTURE

- **CLASSICAL.** Culture in this sense means the highest artistic products of a people: its poetry, its literature, its music, and its artwork. In this sense, some people are "cultured," and others are not. So, if you go to the opera on Saturday night, some people would say you have culture. If you go bowling, some people may think you lack culture. Culture has a normative sense here.

- **MODERN.** Culture in this sense means the unity of language, custom, and territory. Thus, if a people share a common language, have similar customs and material objects, and live within a defined territory, they represent a culture. In this sense, everyone has a culture—you are Mexican, Filipino, African American, etc. Cultures can be seen in smaller units as well: different regions of Mexico, the Philippines, etc. This is the understanding of culture that shapes most of our talk about multicultural or intercultural realities.

- **POSTMODERN.** Especially in urban settings where cultures (in the modern sense just discussed) rub up against one another, people may be speaking their traditional language as well as another language. They may adapt customs of their neighbors. And they don't have their own defined territory. The place in which they find themselves is really a forum where things are borrowed and crafted together to create a way of life. This is what is known as postmodern culture. It is especially prevalent among second- and third-generation immigrants and youth.

⧉ **GROUP ACTIVITIES**

1. Description of "Culture": Distribute two sticky note papers and a colored pen to each participant. Ask participants to write two different words (one on each sticky note) that they associate with the concept of "culture." Ask participants to share their words with tablemates and have participants explain why they chose them.

   In the big group, ask participants to shout out examples of the words mentioned. From the examples, craft a description of what "culture" is.

   Ask participants to group all the words at their respective tables into the three elements of culture—material; action or behavior; and values, beliefs, and attitudes. Ask each table to give examples of the three elements of culture that they have experienced or observed in the American, Chinese, French, or any other culture. Have participants retain their sticky notes for the next activity.

2. Iceberg Concept of Culture: Give a flip chart paper with a sketch of a floating iceberg on it to every table. Ask participants what a common characteristic is of an iceberg and "culture." Request that participants place their words on the sticky notes (from the previous activity) above or below the depicted waterline. Identify cultural attitudes, values, or beliefs that have visible manifestations. For example, in some cultures, a high value for respect of the elderly can be shown through language (use of honorific words) and body language (kissing the hands of the elderly, bowing to the elderly, etc.).

3. The Orange "Take-Out" Box: The orange "take-out" box is a full box of fun and practical items to inspire participation, open-mindedness, feedback, learning, and humor. This box of tools helps learners focus, relax, and absorb information by allowing them to engage in tactile experiences. The predesigned box can be obtained online from the Trainer's Warehouse (*www.trainerswarehouse.com*).

4. In small groups, play "intercultural bingo" by listing numerous distinctive practices, terms, and events of importance to particular cultures in the United States. Then have the small group accurately explain all the items listed. Give a prize to the small group that wins. Reflect on what was learned about one's knowledge of cultures other than one's own.

5. Table Talk 1: Within small groups, have each table participant strive to identify his or her strengths and weaknesses regarding each of the basic components of intercultural competence.

6. Table Talk 2: Each participant completes the column entitled "Implications of Parameters of Intercultural Competence." Within small groups, ask the participants to share their answers and examples of these parameters of interacting with other cultures. As one large group, encourage participants to discuss the implications of their answers in particular pastoral settings as well as possible weaknesses they have noted in themselves.

MODULE 3

*Develop Intercultural Communication Skills
in Pastoral Settings*

GOALS

1. To introduce participants to how groups from collectivist and individualist perspectives see themselves and how they view groups constituted differently from themselves

2. To indicate how these different perceptions affect meetings where groups from different perspectives need to interact

3. To outline some of the cultural features that play into intergroup conflict and how these features might be addressed

OUTCOMES

- Develop practical knowledge about intercultural communications in pastoral settings.

- Increase awareness of how to communicate effectively with persons and groups in cultures other than one's own.

- Use modes of communication that are proper to the culture being addressed.

- Lead, discuss, and make decisions using culturally appropriate processes with intercultural groups.

- Apply basic skills in conflict resolution.

This module takes the material that has been learned in the previous modules and applies it to determine how to work with groups of differing cultures in ministry situations. The module begins by considering how groups look at themselves, and it then examines how groups interact, meet, and make decisions.

The second half of the module introduces participants to the intricacies of dealing with conflict in settings where the differences fall along cultural lines.

How groups see themselves and how they interact with other groups has two particularly important dimensions: (1) whether one's group is more collectivist or individualist in nature and (2) what happens when a predominantly collectivist group and a predominantly individualist group have to interact with one another.

The "Face" of Groups

Face is the public image of a group, or how a group wants others—individuals or groups—to see it. This involves two projects: (1) presenting our face in the way we want others to perceive and interact with us and (2) doing what we need to do within our own group to support that face.

Recall that collectivist cultures often have a stronger sense of hierarchy or high-power distance. Communication is often more indirect ("high context"). Authority and status tend to be inherited. Sanctions and rewards are based on one's social position in the group.

Individualist cultures, on the other hand, are typically more egalitarian and low-power distance. Communication tends to be more direct ("low context").

Authority is to be earned rather than inherited. Sanctions and rewards are based on individual performance rather than social position.

Whether a culture is more collectivist or individualist affects how it regards and maintains its face. In other words, a collectivist or individualist orientation influences how a culture behaves to present itself to others and how it maintains itself.

Stella Ting-Toomey, one of the foremost researchers in this field, has analyzed how face works in "The Matrix of Face: An Updated Face-Negotiation Theory." According to Ting-Toomey, there are three predominant values that shape the face of a group and are particularly important:

- *Autonomy.* My group is self-sufficient and does not need to be tutored or guided by other groups. We do not want to be treated as dependent children.
- *Morality.* My group is likeable, reliable, approachable, and deserves to be included in activities and events. We live by certain values that are good and important.
- *Competence.* My group has resources, achievements, and prized values. These need to be acknowledged and respected by other groups.

In an individualist culture, these three contents of face apply especially to individuals. In a more collectivist culture, they stand out in a particular way for the entire group.

Communication Styles Based on Face Management

As has already been noted, collectivism and hierarchy often correlate in cultures. With that correlation comes a "high context" way of living. In face management, that translates into more indirect modes of verbal communication and a greater use of body language to express feelings and ideas.

In more individualist cultures, because of the likelihood of emphasizing equality and favoring a "low context" way of living, more direct communication tends to prevail, and body language does not play a significant role.

For example, people coming from individualist cultures often have difficulty understanding when "yes" means "yes" and when "yes" means "no" in collectivist cultures. In collectivist cultures, to say "no" to someone of superior rank—especially in face-to-face situations—dishonors them. Thus, people from individualist cultures need to learn the more subtle cues that indicate whether "yes" means "yes" or "yes" means "no."

The use of silence is another form of communication that typically means something different in individualist and collectivist cultures. In individualist cultures, silence is the absence of communication or, alternatively, implicit agreement with what is being said ("silence means consent"). In collectivist cultures, silence can be a powerful mode of communication. It can mean agreement, but it also can mean profound disagreement. (See the discussion of avoidance below.) People in collectivist cultures who have been oppressed by individualist cultures will sometimes test the sincerity of their individualist counterparts. For example, in Native American cultures historically oppressed by Europeans, Native Americans tend to notice how well Europeans are able to remain silent without interrupting Native Americans who are speaking.

Body language is also an important form of communication. In individualist cultures, children being scolded are typically expected to maintain eye contact with their elders as a way of showing respect and sincerity. In many collectivist cultures, however, the exact opposite is expected: the child being scolded is expected to look down and avoid eye contact with their elders.

Another cultural variable is how close or how far away one stands from the person one is speaking with. Proximity can mean either intimacy or seriousness of intention. Distance can mean either respect or disinterest.

The same differentials hold for body contact and modes of greeting. Rules may be different for men and for women within a culture, and how one greets a person of the opposite sex differs among cultures.

Finally, expressions of emotion vary from culture to culture. Giggling may be a sign of agreement or solidarity (especially around something that is perceived as humorous) in individualist cultures, but it is frequently a sign of nervousness in collectivist cultures. Likewise, practices such as weeping in public may have different meanings across cultures.

Conducting Meetings with Differing Cultures

Meetings are part of parish and school life. What some people are not aware of is how much culture can shape meeting and decision-making styles. What follows here contrasts styles of *individualist/equality/low context/long-term time orientation* with styles of *collectivist/hierarchy/high context/short-term time orientation*. These are, of course, exaggerations or ideal types. However, by using them to create a rather stark contrast, one can get a better feel for the distinctive styles that affect meetings and decision making.

Individualist Styles of Meeting and Decision Making

Individualist cultures that work out of a sense of equality and concern for the long term are typically more *task-oriented* when it comes to meetings. Meetings are called for a purpose, and a clear agenda is established ahead of time. Meetings begin and end at prescribed times. If the work of the meeting is finished early, so much the better; people have the advantage of getting away sooner than had been expected.

There are clear rules for how to proceed in a meeting. (People often follow *Robert's Rules of Order*.) It is the task of the person moderating the meeting to keep participants on task and following the rules. To allow more people to speak, sometimes a stipulated time length for any remarks is established at the outset of the meeting.

Everyone is encouraged to speak to the issue within the timeframe allotted. There may be a procedure for determining when there has been enough debate. Ultimately, a vote is taken, with the majority (or other plurality) determining the outcome.

Collectivist Styles of Meeting and Decision Making

Collectivist cultures that work out of hierarchy and demonstrate greater concern for the short term tend to prize the maintenance of good relationships among the participants over the completion of the task. Settling a task too quickly can damage relationships for future meetings. While a time for beginning and ending the meeting may be established ahead of time, the meeting cannot start until everyone has had a chance to greet everyone else and inquire about their families, their health, and the like. When a sense of harmony is in place, the meeting can get under way. Meetings are preferably not ended until harmony is again re-established. This may require some eating and drinking together.

The use of *Robert's Rules of Order* is considered a rather rude way of conducting business, because it does not adequately honor a group's face. Rather, when an item of business is introduced, the elders of the respective groups must each first address the issue before it can be opened up for debate. This somewhat formal way of addressing the issue establishes the face of the group in terms of autonomy, morality, and competence. Moreover, setting time limits on elders' speaking damages face. The task of the moderator of the meeting is to ensure that the face of the various groups is honored before proceeding with debate.

In debate, individuals will speak, but rarely will a member of a group (especially if young) contradict directly anything the elder has said. If a contrary point is to be made, it must be done in a way that reinforces what the elder has said even as a slightly different point is made. Elders must be given a chance to respond and affirm what a member has said so as to show that what appears to be a contrary idea really is not so. In some instances, younger members of the group are expected not to speak at all.

If the moderator wants individuals to ask questions, it is best done by letting the groups gather to discuss the matter among themselves and then letting each group appoint a spokesperson who will present the questions to the larger group. Individuals often will not feel free to speak independently of the group.

When it comes to making a decision, groups will gather with their elders to determine how they will vote. Then the voting can take place. Often, the most important aspect of the decision is that the group is united in presenting its vote.

Respectful Communication and Mutual Invitation

To facilitate sharing and discussion in a diverse group, Eric Law introduced guidelines for respectful communication as well as a mutual invitation process model in the early 1990s in *The Wolf Shall Dwell with the Lamb: A Spirituality for Leadership in a Multicultural Community*. The processes he outlines promote true dialogue when diverse groups encounter one another around a meeting or discussion table. The concept of invitation empowers a person because it is a way of giving power away. Accepting an invitation is a way to claim power. In this way, invitation becomes a spiritual discipline for intercultural relationships.

Leadership and Response to Complex Issues

Beyond procedures, how groups believe leadership should be exercised and the ways in which groups think complex questions should be addressed also may fall along these individualist and collectivist lines.

In individualist settings, leadership is often seen as enabling individuals to bring their talents to bear on issues the community is facing. People will be respected as good leaders if they can demonstrate competence (by citing their training and education) and show their skills in bringing people together to carry out necessary tasks.

In facing complex issues, a good leader is someone who can break down an issue into discrete tasks and develop a timetable for meeting them. Skills in planning and setting goals and objectives are especially prized.

In collectivist cultures, leaders may be chosen based on their rank and status within the community. In such cultures, leadership is more about trustworthiness than specific skills. People will be respected as good leaders if they come from a family that has shown a capacity to keep a community together and promote harmonious relationships. In facing complex tasks, the leader who brings the community along and keeps the community together is more important than a detailed plan. Plans may be articulated, but their purpose is often more to impress outsiders with the competence of the group than to provide a detailed guide of how to get to the desired end.

Discussion

Clearly, both meeting and leadership styles have advantages. If one starts from a task orientation, as individualist cultures often do, satisfaction arises from getting the task accomplished. If one begins with a relationship

---

RESPECTFUL COMMUNICATION GUIDELINE

R: take **RESPONSIBILITY** for what you say and feel, and speak with words others can hear and understand

E: use **EMPATHETIC** listening, not just words but also feelings being expressed, non-verbal language including silence

S: be **SENSITIVE** to differences in communication styles

P: **PONDER** on what you hear and feel before you speak

E: **EXAMINE** your own assumptions and perceptions

C: keep **CONFIDENTIALITY**

T: **TRUST** the process because we are *not* here to debate who is right or wrong but to experience true dialogue

---

orientation, as collectivist cultures often do, satisfaction arises from maintaining good relationships with everyone.

Both styles also have disadvantages. A task-oriented approach can trample on the feelings of some of the participants. A relationship-oriented approach can go on and on and never complete what needs to be done.

Dealing with Conflicts in the Community

Conflicts are a natural part of human interaction. Conflict is not always an entirely negative experience; sometimes very constructive things can come from resolving a conflict. The following information shows how culture influences the way we deal with conflict. Again, the individualist-collectivist typology will be used.

The perspectives of *self* and *other* are important in examining conflicts: What do I see myself trying to do in the conflict? What do I see the other as trying to do? It is also helpful here to refer back to the discussion of *face* from the previous session. Individualist cultures are concerned principally about individual face over the face of the group. Collectivist cultures are more concerned with the face of the group than individual face.

Individualist Approaches to Conflict

Following the previous discussion about meetings, individualist approaches will often frame conflict in terms of the *issues* at stake, although relationships may be heavily involved. The concern in conflict is to resolve the issue. The mode of communication is typically a direct one rather than an indirect one. Individualist approaches may rely on a strategy of *dominating* the other in order to win. In some circumstances, these approaches will adopt a policy of *compromise*, with the intention of later returning to the conflict when conditions are more favorable for winning.

Collectivist Approaches to Conflict

Collectivist approaches may frame the conflict in terms of issues, but relationships—especially regarding group face—are always key in the strategies involved. The concern in the conflict is to maintain good group face. Because hierarchical patterns of organization are in place, the preferred mode of communication is indirect rather than direct. There is a tendency to choose strategies of *avoidance* rather than risk loss of face. If avoidance is not possible, *obliging* the other party will be an alternative. The conflict is then not resolved but

allowed to continue, albeit implicitly and indirectly, so that it makes resolved relationships difficult to achieve. By refusing to re-engage the conflict, a dispute may go on into the next generation.

According to Ting-Toomey and her colleagues, a range of behaviors (verbal or nonverbal) are employed in conflict situations to defuse, aggravate, repair damaged image, restore face loss, or heal broken relationships. These behaviors are referred to as *facework*.

Discussion

Bringing a community together where individualist and collectivist approaches are in play at the same time can be difficult. Because conflict can involve both issues and relationships, there is a likelihood that strategies will veer back and forth between these two foci.

In addition, *contextual* issues can be at stake as well. Sometimes in immigrant and minority communities, church settings may be the only places where a group's autonomy and competence face has a chance of being respected. What is happening to the immigrant or minority group outside the church circle in everyday life will constantly invade disputes within the church. This is most evident where two groups are struggling for control in the same parish—be it over Mass schedules, use of space, or whose saints and Madonnas will be honored. Hence, keeping *external context*, *issues*, and *relationships* in mind is an important component of successful conflict resolution.

FACEWORK

A **dominating facework** can include defensive and aggressive behaviors like yelling, credentialing, and a competitive one-up/one-down strategy that pushes for a group's own position or objective above and beyond the other group's position or interest.

Avoiding facework emphasizes the preservation of relationship and harmony, and it uses the following strategies: making excuses, not directly confronting conflict, avoiding contact with the other group, obliging or giving in to the other group, pretending to gloss over the conflict, and seeking the help of an intermediary or third party.

Integrating facework addresses both the issue resolution and the preservation of relationship and harmony. Some strategies that promote mutual face-saving are remaining calm, mindful listening, apologizing, compromising, intentional reframing, practicing collaborative dialogue, and problem solving.

# RESORCES

Cushner, Kenneth, and Richard W. Brislin (eds.). *Improving Intercultural Interactions: Module for Cross-Cultural Training Programs: Volume 2*. Thousand Oaks, CA: Sage Publications, 1979.

Gudykunst, William B. (ed.). *Theorizing About Intercultural Communication*. Thousand Oaks, CA: Sage Publications, 2005.

Law, Eric H. F. *The Wolf Shall Dwell with the Lamb: A Spirituality for Leadership in a Multicultural Community*. St. Louis, MO: Chalice Press, 1993.

Peace Corps. *Culture Matters: The Peace Corps Cross-Cultural Workbook*. Washington, DC: Peace Corps Information Collection and Exchange, 1997.

Ting-Toomey, Stella. "The Matrix of Face: An Updated Face-Negotiation Theory." In *Theorizing About Cultural Competence*, edited by William B. Gudykunst. Thousand Oaks, CA: Sage Publications, 2005.

USCCB. *Who Are My Sisters and Brothers? A Catholic Educational Guide for Understanding and Welcoming Immigrants and Refugees*. Washington, DC: USCCB, 1996.

USCCB. *Who Are My Sisters and Brothers? Understanding and Welcoming Immigrants and Refugees*. (Videotape). Washington, DC: USCCB, 1996.

GROUP ACTIVITIES

1. What is "face" and "facework"? Solicit from participants what their understanding of "face" is. Why is it important to understand the dynamic of "face" in intercultural communication? Similarly, ask participants if they have heard about "facework" and its value to intercultural communication.

2. In the Mind of the Beholder: This activity is a quick introduction to language (verbal and nonverbal). Distribute the handout and proceed with the exercise. The facilitator demonstrates the first three gestures. Discuss the various possible interpretations of the sample gestures and the verbal message in the exercise.

3. Four Factors to Consider When Working with Intercultural Groups: Provide a brief overview of the four factors: communication styles, meetings and decision making, leadership, and dealing with conflict.

Explain the table talk exercise. Each table will discuss one of the four factors by reflecting on the two questions assigned to the particular table. Distribute the reflection questions. Remind the groups about the mutual invitation process and respectful communication principles. Each group is to select a reporter who will take notes on the highlights of the table discussion and then give a five-minute summary of the discussion to the larger group.

The facilitator assigns a factor to each table. After the fifteen-minute table talk, the facilitator asks each table to report. After reports are given about each of the factors, the facilitator highlights a couple points mentioned by each reporter and provides a PowerPoint summary about the significant features of each of the four group communication factors.

FACE VALUES

- **Autonomy.** My group is self-sufficient and does not need to be tutored or guided by other groups. We do not want to be treated as dependent children.

- **Morality.** My group is likeable, reliable, approachable, and deserves to be included in activities and events. We live by certain values that are good and important.

- **Competence.** My group has resources, achievements, and prized values. These need to be acknowledged and respected by other groups.

MODULE 4

Expand Knowledge of the Obstacles That Impede Effective Intercultural Relations

 **GOALS**

1. To identify the processes of in-group and out-group perception and behavior
2. To examine the ways we view the "other"
3. To explore the dynamics of racism and better understand its effects on its victims
4. To learn how to positively influence the healthy dynamics of living together in community

 **OUTCOMES**

- Increased awareness of the presence of racism in intercultural relationships and how it affects those relationships
- Increased knowledge and understanding of racism
- Renewed willingness to confront one's own experiences of racism
- Acknowledgement and ownership of one's feelings about racism
- Strengthened resolve to find one's voice to speak out against racism

This module addresses some of the obstacles to appropriate and effective intercultural communication in ministry. It focuses on the processes of prejudice—that is, how we stereotype the "other." The module then explores the dynamics of racism. It also provides insight into how we can move from ethnocentrism (solely focusing on our own group as normative for society) to healthy interaction between ethnically and culturally diverse groups.

The Dynamics of Prejudice and Stereotypes

Prejudice involves thinking differently about those outside our own group in one or more negative ways. Infants do not discriminate against other infants who are different from themselves. Discrimination is something that we learn from our culture.

According to evolutionary biologists, prejudice is interwoven with very old instincts in group behavior that go back some ten thousand years, to the time when people lived in small groups of hunter-gatherers. Fear of outsiders and groups other than our own was often warranted, because the other group could attack and harm us. This idea conforms to the Darwinian understanding of nature as being merely "survival of the fittest," but recent research suggests that cooperation was as important among our ancestors as competition and protection (see R. Axelrod, *The Evolution of Cooperation* [New York: Basic Books, 1985]).

Our goal in the following portion of the module is to examine how negative reactions to outside groups occur and manifest themselves.

In-Group and Out-Group Dynamics

Contact with people unknown to us often triggers the dynamics of in-group and out-group formation. The "in-group" is made up of people we know and trust and people we deem to be most like us. With the in-group, we feel relatively safe. Those we do not know or trust and those who seem different from ourselves in whatever way (e.g., skin color, language, customs) constitute the "out-group."

We judge these individuals by different standards than those we use for our own group. Thus, if someone in our own group does something wrong, we are more likely to condone the deed or attribute it to outside factors. The 1970s comedian Flip Wilson's famous line "The devil made me do it!" is an example of shifting the blame away from ourselves.

However, when someone in the out-group does something bad or wrong, we are more likely to attribute it to malevolence: that person did something wrong because he or she wanted to do it.

Psychologists call this willingness to think badly of other people "projection" because we project our negative feelings (or even things we do not want to admit to ourselves that we do) onto the unknown "others."

When we feel insecure or under threat, our suspicions about the out-group intensify, and we are more willing to make quick judgments about them.

Here are some examples of common projections onto the "other":

- *"They are dirty."* They do not maintain proper hygiene. Their food would be dangerous for us to eat. We should not have contact with them for fear of picking up some disease.
- *"They are lazy."* They do not have the same habits and values that we have, so they are not to be trusted. We must keep our distance from them.
- *"They can't control their emotions."* They are aggressive and dangerous. They cannot control their sexual impulses. They do not keep proper boundaries.

Specific Ways We Judge the "Other"

Jesus enjoined us to love our neighbors as ourselves. This is a considerable challenge, because it seems we are generally unable to see the "others" as ourselves. This may be because we do not ever entirely know ourselves, and our own uncertainties end up getting projected on those we do not know. It may also be a way of protecting ourselves from the unknown.

UNDERSTANDING AND PROCESSING RACISM

1. Identify racial anxiety as the culturally learned behavior that cripples intercultural leadership from casting its gaze on "the elephant in the center of the living room" of the intercultural/multicultural discussion.

2. Briefly review how cultural anxiety affects the intercultural leader's ability to speak about his or her reality.

3. Suggest a means of developing the intercultural leader's capacities to assist others on the path to leadership within the cultural context of white privilege.

4. Present a framework for intercultural engagement that includes white privilege as a useful concept within the dialogue, and also suggest the pertinence of other variables (e.g., gender and social class) that sometimes are relegated to the margins of the intercultural dialogue.

5. Demonstrate the transformative effect of group learning that arises from expressing and sharing the reality of racism as a lived experience among diverse racial, ethnic, and cultural communities.

Here are some of the common ways of dealing with the "other" in this manner:

- *We generalize about them:* "All those people are exactly the same." We recognize a great deal of difference and variation within our own in-group, yet we can make the broadest generalizations about members of the out-group. We can even lump all out-groups together through the use of negative stereotypes about them.
- *We demonize them:* We treat them as dangerous and out to get us. They are powerful and to be feared and are plotting against us. Consequently, they should be excluded from society. We, on the other hand, are kind and benevolent. But they wish to take advantage of our kindness and benevolence to ultimately take away what is dear to us.
- *We see them as helpless children:* They are all poorly educated and are simpletons. Hence, they need our guidance and direction. In this way, we colonize the other: we rescue them from their ignorance by our benign power over them.
- *We trivialize painful differences:* We refuse to recognize neuralgic points that divide groups against one another. For example, some Caucasians tell African Americans that they are color-blind and treat everyone alike, regardless of race, but their behavior toward African Americans tells another story. Trivialization is a way of refusing to acknowledge how differences divide people.
- *We make them invisible:* We refuse to acknowledge their presence and treat them as if they were not there. Think of Ralph Ellison's classic book *Invisible Man*.

There are additional ways in which we judge the "others," but these are the most characteristic, especially within powerful in-groups.

The Reality of Racism

This section of the module addresses the challenge of talking about racism in secular and Church circles because of shared cultural anxiety about the subject. In their pastoral letter titled *Brothers and Sisters to Us*, the Catholic bishops of the United States reflect on the reality of racism, which unfortunately exists in the Church as a human—and thus sinful—institution in need of conversion as well as in secular society. Consequently, Catholic leaders need to develop the skill of finding their "voice," or the words appropriate for capturing the reality of racism. They are called upon to give insightful, effective, and reconciling guidance in the sanctuary and the streets.

This module on race and racial privilege frames its content around the scriptural precedent in the early Christian community of identifying racism as a by-product of racial privilege. This frame of reference is transferred to the present reality we find in our church community, which mirrors the cultural dynamics of European American, Latino, Asian, and Native American responses to the culture of white privilege in everyday America. This module discusses the dynamics of ethnocentrism as the energy of a particular form of privilege by the in-group having the power to define by description as well as the power to determine how to regard and treat those who are the "others." Racial privilege in America today is characterized by the regulating of Church and society to maintain, advance, and secure the future of white privilege over and against the "nonwhite others" who make up the out-group.

Intercultural Leaders with Voices That Capture the Reality of Racism

The challenge before us to deal with various kinds of racisms is as old as the Church. Racism, as used in this context, is a social dysfunction in which people do not see others as their brothers and sisters in the same human family. *Racism* denotes the reality that there are many ways of depersonalizing people as the "others," not just one means. There is the "otherness" of race, gender, class, religion, ethnicity, and culture. Let us begin our experience with a reading from our family history as Christians as we engage our present reality. This reading is used as an example of the timelessness of the human struggle in dealing with matters of racial diversity.

St. Paul's Letter to the Galatians, particularly 2:1-13 and 3:27-29, provides a clear illustration of how racial and cultural diversity was a source of controversy for the Church in its infancy. St. Paul confronts and reproaches St. Peter for not consistently following the understanding the Church had come to regarding the evangelization of the Gentiles. This episode reveals that part of the challenge of cultural diversity in the Church is to not deny that we who are framing the question are also influenced by the unperceived racism around us. As members of our cultures, we are directed to effectively deny this challenge by simply imposing a "Don't Talk" rule:

- We must not talk about race.
- We ought to deny any feelings that we have regarding race.
- We should not trust ourselves with the subject.

How do we as leaders in the Church break the "Don't Talk" rule and transform the proverbial elephant in the room into a house pet? We begin by developing the cultural competence to find our voice in a racialized culture. We begin by practicing the "Do Talk" rule:

- We must talk about race.
- We ought to express our feelings about race.
- We should trust our own efforts to express the reality of racism to guide our journey.

To begin our journey and growth in competency, we have to find our voice. Our first exercise to find our voice in opposition to racism calls for us to identify the obstacles. The FIG Complex was developed by Fr. Boniface Hardin, OSB, to assist those seeking to free themselves from racial anxiety when discussing racial issues. Fr. Hardin sees that our racial anxiety arises from three areas: fear, ignorance, and guilt—thus, the FIG Complex.

Framing Intercultural Conversations on Diversity and Race

Intercultural leaders are called to move beyond fear and anxiety as they lead the Body of Christ into the beloved

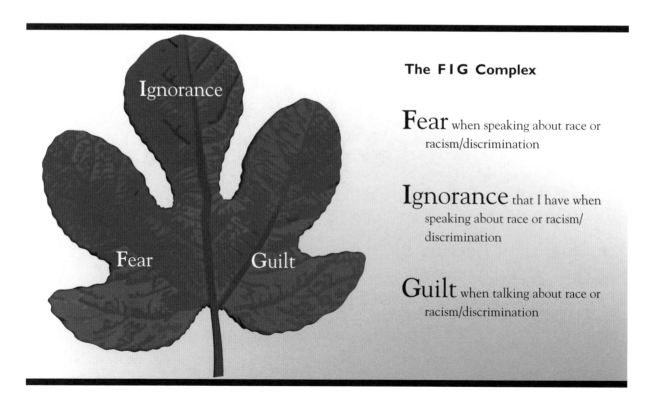

The FIG Complex

Fear when speaking about race or racism/discrimination

Ignorance that I have when speaking about race or racism/discrimination

Guilt when talking about race or racism/discrimination

community of the Fatherhood of God. This is the work of the Gospel that all disciples of Jesus are called to in our day. When we find our voice for expressing the reality of racism, we fulfill the prayer of Jesus in the Gospel of John: " . . . so that they may be one just as we are" (Jn 17:11).

Framing Our Terms as We Find Our Voice

- The term "multicultural" frames the conversation with terms supplied by the White Anglo-Saxon Protestant (WASP) context of the racial "other."
- "Multicultural" became the umbrella to collect "non-white" realities and avoid the four-letter "*r-a-c-e*" word for whites and non-whites alike in our "Don't Talk" culture.
- Consequently, a conversation about diversity begins with the assumption that one's social representation in the cultures of the Americas starts with racial framing in a U.S. culture that is strongly influenced by white privilege.
- The leader in the field of diversity, however, goes beyond the "multicultural" framing of the question. Such a leader possesses a dual awareness of his or her own cultural description provided by white privilege as well as how he or she simultaneously participates in numerous diverse cultures that are described within the larger context.

In the second chapter of Galatians, St. Paul criticizes St. Peter for his ethnocentrism against the Gentile converts and his hypocrisy in regarding them as the "other." He reminds Peter that we are reborn in Christ, not as Jews and Gentiles but as people of a new creation. This kind of conflict threatened the future existence of the Church; it can and does do the same damage today if left unchecked by leaders. The plurality of racial groups in U.S. society will require a pluricultural lens to build the bridges of interculturality. Leaders who have found their voice have assisted the Church in playing its proper role and in overcoming cultural, racial, and ethnic barriers. Intercultural leaders of the twenty-first century will find St. Paul to be a role model for identifying and naming the reality of racism as well as building bridges between all God's children.

RESOURCES

Massingale, Bryan N. *Racial Justice and the Catholic Church*. Maryknoll, NY: Orbis Books, 2010.

USCCB. *Brothers and Sisters to Us: United States Bishops Pastoral Letter on Racism in Our Day*. Washington, DC: USCCB, 1979.

USCCB. *For the Love of One Another*: Special Message on the Occasion of the Tenth Anniversary of *Brothers and Sisters to Us*. Washington, DC: Bishops' Committee on Black Catholics, 1989.

Williams, Clarence. "Beyond Multiculturalism: Engaging Pluricultural Ministry." *CHURCH Magazine*, vol. 24, no. 2 (Summer 2008).

Williams, Clarence. *Racial Sobriety: Becoming the Change You Want to See*. Detroit, MI: Institute for Recovery from Racisms, n.d.

GROUP ACTIVITIES

1. Begin a small group discussion of Galatians 2:1-13 and 3:27-29. Encourage participants to share their personal experiences with matters of race in parish, diocesan, school, or organizational contexts.

2. Review pertinent sections of the following pastoral letters on racism by the Catholic bishops of the United States: *Brothers and Sisters to Us* and *For the Love of One Another*. Ask participants to share their reflections and concerns with the larger group.

MODULE 5

Foster Ecclesial Integration Rather Than Assimilation in Church Settings with a Spirituality of Hospitality, Reconciliation, and Mission

 ## GOALS

1. To experience a spirituality that supports intercultural ministry and reconciliation
2. To focus on the developmental process for ecclesial integration and inclusion, specifically in diverse parish settings, including competencies for
   - Building relationships
   - Effective communication
   - Decision making
3. To identify models for effective pastoral responses, principles, and practices that shape fruitful ministry in intercultural settings

 ## OUTCOMES

- Demonstrate a clear understanding of the principle of *ecclesial integration* versus *assimilation*.
- Identify different parish models in the context of cultural diversity and a spirituality of mission and reconciliation.
- Apply the developmental process of *ecclesial integration* and its five principles to one's own parish or Catholic institution.

This module offers an appropriate spirituality to support intercultural ministries and practical applications. It includes a developmental process for ecclesial integration, intercultural relationships, and stewardship. The process shows how parish members reach a new sense of Catholic identity, belonging, and ownership. The module also explores generational differences among new immigrants and offers pastoral principles to develop effective intercultural ministries.

The module is written mostly from the perspective of the new immigrants and the communities that receive them. However, for the purpose of our study of ecclesial integration, where it says "immigrant," it can also be read "newcomer."

There may be cases where those new to the parish family or to the neighborhood are not necessarily immigrants from other countries but members of other ethnic, racial, or cultural groups. It may also be the case that the "newcomers" are members of a community that has always "been there," but they were either neglected or ignored and now ask for inclusion.

Spirituality for Intercultural Ministry and Reconciliation

For intercultural ministry to be effective, it will need a lived spirituality to support it. It is one thing to have knowledge, ability, and skills in the area of intercultural relations, but it is quite another to be motivated to act on what one knows. The Church embodies a spirituality of *encounter, conversion, communion, solidarity,* and *mission.* Pope John Paul II's apostolic exhortation *Ecclesia in America* articulates this spirituality.

The Methodology of "The Church in America"

- *Catholic identity:* Encounter with Christ leading to conversion, which means to "turn one's mind and heart around."
- *Communion:* The communion of the Church, rooted in God's love, offers all people the sense of identity, purpose, and community they seek.
- *Solidarity:* A firm and persevering determination to commit oneself (and a whole faith community) to the common good.

The "Going Fishing" Response

A particularly poignant example of how pastoral ministers sometimes remain paralyzed in the face of new challenges like the ones posed by diversity is found in Chapter 21 of St. John's Gospel. We read about the encounter of the disciples with Jesus after his Resurrection and learn how he made breakfast for them.

Discouraged by the loss of their Master, the disciples try to go back to what they did before they met Jesus. In today's multicultural context, parish leaders may also experience the "Going Fishing" response:

- The parish leadership may feel
  † Discouraged because many new immigrant Catholics living around them do not go to Mass or participate in parish activities
  † Uneasy about the presence of new immigrants and wonder if they are "illegals"
- New immigrants feel discouraged by
  † Their difficult situation as foreigners in a foreign land
  † Economic, family, and immigration issues
  † The Catholic parish's doors remaining closed to them (i.e., nothing is offered in their language, access to parish facilities is denied, their faith symbols are not welcome in the church, or they are relegated to worship in the basement)

Encounter

Daylight breaks. A stranger appears on the shore and asks them about their fishing in a caring and familiar tone. By doing this, Jesus helps them break the cycle of their obsession.

One example:

- Parish leadership
  † Is obsessed with expecting new immigrants to just come through the door and fit in—speak English, assimilate, and "be like us"
- New immigrants
  † Are homesick
  † Sometimes feel that they deserve to be excluded

An encounter with the Living Jesus Christ is the point of departure for Christian discipleship. Some encounters with Jesus mentioned in the Gospel are clearly personal, as when Jesus summons someone to follow him (Mt 9:9; Mk 2:13-14; Lk 5:27-28). In these cases, Jesus deals with familiarity with his hearers: "Rabbi, where are you staying? . . . Come and see." In other cases, the encounters are communal in nature, as when Jesus spoke to the Twelve: "To you it has been given to know the secrets of the kingdom of heaven, but to them it has not been given" (Mt 13:11). The Church is the place where men and women, by encountering Jesus, can come to know the love of the Father (Jn 14:9) through the powerful agency of the Holy Spirit, transforming believers and giving them new life.

Conversion

It is only when they lower the nets on the other side, when they are free from their obsession, that they are able to recognize who has been standing on the shore.

One example:

- Parish leadership realizes that
  † The presence of new immigrants in their midst is a blessing from God
  † They need to reach out to them, for Jesus is also present among them
  † Their call to go out and make disciples is rekindled
- New immigrants
  † Free themselves from thinking only about their economic needs and from their homesick state of mind
  † Begin to seek God, rekindling their hope for the Good News

Conversion was at the heart of Jesus' message. Conversion, or *metanoia* in Greek, means "to turn one's mind around." This means turning away from sin and turning toward God. In an intercultural ministry, we turn away from the sins of racism and prejudice. We turn toward the image and likeness of God to be found in each human being, including the "other" and those who are "different." The New Testament stories of the Good Samaritan (Lk 10:25-37) and Jesus' encounters with the Syro-Phoenician woman (Mk 7:24-30) and the Samaritan woman (Jn 4:4-42) are examples of what intercultural ministry should be trying to do.

Conversion means both a conversion of our hearts and the conversion of those social structures and biases that perpetuate racism and discrimination.

Communion

Jesus becomes the gracious host, cooking for them and inviting them to contribute their own newly caught fish.

- Parish leaders follow Jesus' example as gracious hosts by welcoming the new immigrant community; taking into account their culture, language, expectations, and contributions; and realizing that the "guests" should soon become "hosts" like them.
- New immigrants feel at home in an environment of trust, kindness, and safety.

The communion of the Church, rooted in God's love, is called to offer all people the sense of identity, purpose, and community they seek. Claimed by Christ and baptized into the Holy Spirit, Catholic people from all generations, cultures, races, immigration statuses, and social situations have become full members of the Church, and all are worthy of the love, the respect, and the support of the entire Christian community. In a society that is increasingly diverse and to some extent divided, we must urgently proclaim with joy and firm faith that through our "communion with Christ . . . we enter into living communion with all believers" (*Ecclesia in America*, no. 33). Living out a theology of communion entails creating greater harmony among peoples. It does not call for the erasure of difference; rather, it brings differences into harmony with one another. An intercultural ministry must be one that welcomes the stranger and works out of an understanding of the Church as communion in which collaboration is central to pastoral service (what in Hispanic ministry is understood as *pastoral de conjunto*). As such, it is a manifestation of the catholicity of the Church.

Solidarity

Jesus asks Simon, son of John, "Do you love me?"

- Jesus reconnects the parish leadership to himself and to the community, more specifically to new immigrants.
- They overcome stereotypes and fear by getting to know new immigrants and recognizing each of them as one of their own.
- Parish leaders rediscover that the victim is made in the image and likeness of God and is therefore of inestimable value.
- Jesus reconnects new immigrants to himself and to the community, ending the isolation that severs trust.
- Jesus empowers new immigrants to reclaim their self-worth.
- God's grace restores their humanity.

Pope John Paul II defines the virtue of solidarity as "a firm and persevering determination to commit oneself [and a whole faith community] to the common good; that is to say to the good of all and of each individual, because we are all really responsible for all" (*Sollicitudo Rei Socialis*, no. 38). This understanding of solidarity is based on the belief in the sanctity of human life and the inherent dignity of every human person, which is deeply rooted in the Gospel and articulated in Catholic social teaching. Solidarity is manifested in a special way in advocacy: for immigrants and the poor, for respect for life from conception to natural death, against discrimination, for the integrity of families, and for justice and peace in a globalized world.

Mission

Jesus commissions Simon Peter by telling him to feed his sheep. Once again, Peter is the Rock upon which the community is built. Peter's vocation to care for Jesus' flock allows him to remember his own past in a different way and to help create a community where trust is nurtured so that denial will never happen again.

- All members of the parish community, both well-established and new arrivals, are fully aware that they are called to take care of one another.
- From their separate stories and narratives, they begin to generate a common narrative that is

centered in the grace of the Resurrection and our experience of reconciliation.

- We all partake in what God has done for us in Christ.

The burning desire to invite others to encounter the Living Jesus Christ is the start of the evangelizing mission to which every Catholic is called. This mission is the grace and vocation proper to the Church and her most profound identity (see *Ecclesia in America*, no. 68).

The entire Church is missionary by its very nature. Each baptized person is called to missionary discipleship of Jesus Christ. This means reaching out and establishing relationships with others, especially those on the margins of society, the poor, and the forgotten. Bringing the Good News to an increasingly culturally diverse population takes us out of the church building, the parish facilities, and the weekly meetings of parish groups. It moves us from pews to shoes to go two by two into the public schools, the neighborhoods, the workplace, the movie theaters, the dance halls, the labor camps, and wherever else Catholic people gather.

Reconciliation as Spirituality for Intercultural Contexts

We all have been victims and wrongdoers at some point in our lives. Intercultural contexts can sometimes give rise to situations in which people feel they have been wronged, treated unfairly, or dehumanized. That is why reconciliation is an integral part of our identity and well-being—of our very lives as Christians.

In *The Ministry of Reconciliation: Spirituality and Strategies*, Fr. Robert J. Schreiter offers the following observation on the nature of reconciliation from a Christian perspective:

> First of all, *reconciliation is the work of God, who initiates and completes in us reconciliation through Christ.* Ultimately, reconciliation is not a human achievement, but the work of God. Furthermore, God initiates the work of reconciliation in the lives of the victims. Ordinarily we would expect reconciliation to begin with the repentance of the wrongdoers. But experience shows that wrongdoers are rarely willing to acknowledge what they have done or come forward of their own accord. If reconciliation

depended entirely upon the wrongdoers' initiative, there would be next to no reconciliation at all.

God begins with the victim, restoring to the victim the humanity which the wrongdoer has tried to wrest away or to destroy. This restoration of humanity might be considered the very heart of reconciliation. The experience of reconciliation is the experience of grace—the restoration of one's damaged humanity in a life-giving relationship with God. Humans are created in the image and likeness of God (Gn 1:26). It is that image by which humanity might mirror divinity, by which humanity comes into communion with divinity, which is restored. That God would begin with the victim, and not the evildoer, is consistent with divine activity in history. God takes the side of the poor, the widowed and the orphaned, the oppressed, the marginal and the imprisoned. It is in the ultimate victim, God's son Jesus Christ, that God begins the process that leads to the reconciliation of the whole world to its Creator and Lord in Christ (Col 1:20).

In like manner, God begins the process of human reconciliation with the victim. It is through the victim that the wrongdoer is called to repentance and forgiveness. Seen from this perspective, repentance and forgiveness are not the preconditions for reconciliation, but are rather the consequences of it.

Models for Ministry in Shared and Intercultural Parishes

Parish life provides different approaches for immigrants to adapt to the prevailing culture within the Church and in society. Instituto Fe y Vida has identified some useful and currently employed parish models, namely Americanizing, personal/ethnic, inclusive, segmented, mission outreach, and integrated.

In the *Americanizing parish*, newcomers are welcome, but they are expected to adapt to the language and culture of the dominant group. Consequently, the parish staff need not gain special language and intercultural communication skills. Newcomers, however, do not feel welcome and experience alienation.

In the *personal/ethnic parish*, the community is served in its particular cultural context and language; leadership and parish staff reflect the culture of the parish; and people from other cultural groups do not participate in these parishes for the most part.

In the *inclusive parish*, newcomers are welcome, and some measure of accommodation is exercised regarding the music, cultural traditions, and celebrations of the immigrant group.

In the *segmented parish*, the parish becomes one of parallel communities, each of which has its own staff.

In the *mission outreach parish*, the predominant group tries to reach out to the other cultural groups, and so it develops some language and intercultural communication skills.

In the *integrated parish*, all cultural groups are equitably and suitably served. There will be residual resentment on the part of the various groups, and some groups will need help embracing such integration.

These parish models constitute a developmental continuum rather than separate modalities. This process is propelled by a spirituality of hospitality, reconciliation, and mission, and it presents four major thresholds: *welcoming*, *Catholic identity*, *sense of belonging*, and *sense of ownership*. Each threshold has movements or steps and requires certain communication competencies.

Ministry with new immigrant communities seeks the healthy inclusion or integration of newcomers into the life and mission of the Church, particularly the parish. In a recent study, CARA shows that 33 percent of parishes in the United States celebrate Mass in a language other than English, compared with 22 percent in 2000 ("U.S. Catholic Parishes Grow in Size and Diversity," *The CARA Report* 16:3 [Winter 2011]). The great majority of these parishes are "shared" by two or more distinct cultural/ethnic communities. The shared parish model strives to achieve a high level of ecclesial integration among its diverse members in a spirit of unity in diversity.

Ecclesial Integration and Inclusion versus Assimilation

"Integration is not to be confused with assimilation. Through the policy of assimilation, new immigrants are forced to give up their language, culture, values, and traditions . . . By [*ecclesial*] integration we mean that [all *cultural/ethnic communities*] are to be welcomed to our church institutions at all levels. They are to be served in their language when possible, and their cultural values and religious traditions are to be respected. Beyond that, we must work toward mutual enrichment through interaction among all our cultures."

—*National Pastoral Plan for Hispanic Ministry*, no. 4

The Process for Ecclesial Integration and Inclusion

Here are foundational stages in the larger process of ecclesial integration:

Catholic Identity
Movement 1: Reach Out and Meet People Where They Are

- **Mission:** Visit them with the Good News of Christ.
- **Affirmation:** Affirm their gifts and contributions.
- **Invitation:** Invite them to the faith community as a home away from home.

Movement 2: Demonstrate Hospitality and Make People Feel at Home

- **Welcoming:** Give them the ecclesial space to be themselves.
- **Identity:** Give them room to develop their own sense of identity.
- **Trust and Safety:** Enable them to adapt to a different culture from a position of strength.

Movement 3: Organize by Developing Ministries and Ministers

- **Opportunity:** They provide for their own ministerial needs and aspirations.
- **Support:** Parish staff and leaders work with them to develop a comprehensive ministry.
- **Room to Grow:** Ministries include the four dimensions of Christian life modeled in the first Christian communities (Acts 2:42-47) and explained in *Encuentro and Mission* (*Living the Present with Enthusiasm*, no. 28).

Belonging

Movement 4: Build Relationships Across Cultures and Ministries

- **Community:** Share their stories, religious traditions, and cultural richness with one another.
- **Celebration:** Celebrate faith and life together with other ministries and cultures.
- **Relationships:** Build relationships, community, and unity between different cultural groups and ministries of the parish.

Movement 5: Champion Leadership Development and Formation

- **Mentoring:** Learn and seek opportunities for ongoing faith formation and training for ministry.
- **Access:** Invest time and talent in certificates and degree programs that are accessible.
- **Recognition:** The entire parish community recognizes and supports newcomers in their ministerial roles.

Movement 6: Open Wide the Doors to the Decision-Making Process

- **Decisions:** Provide space at the table where decisions are made on culturally specific ministries.
- **Leadership:** Encourage an active voice on the life and direction of the faith community as a whole.
- **Representation:** Encourage a place in ministry leadership, parish staff, and other decision-making groups.

Ownership

Movement 7: Strengthen a Sense of Ownership

- **Discernment:** Determine meaningful ways to be involved in the life of the faith community.
- **Solidarity:** Work toward responsiveness from all parish staff on the needs and aspirations of their families and communities.
- **Authority:** Parish leadership and structure recognize newcomers as members on equal terms.

Movement 8: Sow and Reap Full Ownership and Stewardship

- **Shared Responsibility:** Newcomers contribute time, talent, and treasure.
- **Inclusivity:** All parish members build a culturally diverse faith community that is their own.
- **Discipleship:** Newcomers are active participants of a community of faith in which all cultures are constantly transformed by gospel values to be leaven for the Kingdom of God in society.

Movement 9: Achieve Full Commitment to the Mission of the Parish

- **Unity:** Strengthen the unity of the parish while honoring its diversity.
- **Mission:** Be alert and ready to invite and welcome newcomers.
- **Universality:** Become "gente-puente" (a bridge-building people) by ministering with Catholics of all cultural backgrounds.

Intergenerational Communication Among Immigrant Communities

Along with the dynamics of intercultural communication that have already been explored in this module, there is a pattern found in immigrant communities that cuts across other particularities. This pattern involves the stances taken in first and second generations.

"First-generation" people are those who immigrate in adulthood. Their life patterns and language skills are already well in place before they arrive in a new land.

"Second-generation" people include those who arrive in the new country as infants or children and those who are born in the new country. Their developmental patterns and language capacity are shaped by the new country more than those of the first generation.

Because their developmental years are already behind them, the first generation tends to view and interact with the new culture through the lens of their home country. They will often struggle to keep those values and to transmit them to their children.

The second generation finds itself caught between the world of their parents and the culture of the land where they are growing up. This may lead to conflict at home with their parents. They sometimes do not speak the language of their parents well, and they find themselves preferring to speak the language of the new country. They may reject patterns of the parents' culture (such as having their marriage partner or their profession chosen by their parents). This is especially the case when the home culture of their parents is collectivist, and the children find themselves living in a predominantly individualist culture.

Outside the home, the second generation may not receive acceptance from their peers because they are "different." They may speak the language of the dominant culture with a slightly foreign accent. They may be profiled as "foreign." Being caught in between cultures can create special challenges for the second generation, particularly during adolescence and early adulthood as their adult identities begin to coalesce. This reality poses significant challenges for youth and young adult ministries in immigrant settings.

Effects of this conflict are sometimes seen in the third generation (i.e., the children of the second generation), especially when the second generation has tried to jettison the cultural identity of their immigrant parents. The third generation may become especially interested in the culture and even the language of their grandparents, causing tension between the third and the second generation.

Language is always an important factor, and it is an index of where the first and the second generation locate themselves vis-à-vis the two cultures.

These generational differences pose unique concerns for youth and young adult ministries and Catholic educational systems in immigrant settings.

Five Principles for Achieving Ecclesial Integration and Inclusion

1. Articulate a vision of ministry based on ecclesial integration and inclusion:
    *   Recognize and affirm cultural, linguistic, and racial differences as a gift from God, not a problem to be solved.
    *   Promote the formation of culturally specific ministries, parish groups, and apostolic movements as a means for conversion and community building.
    *   Avoid the temptation to expect others to assimilate into a one-size-fits-all youth group, program, or activity.

2. Foster the inculturation of the Gospel in all cultures:
    *   Be aware of your own cultural heritage.
    *   Use the concept of *inculturation* of the Gospel.
    *   Be willing to be a *bridge-builder* rather than a gate-keeper.
    *   Avoid the tendency to see your culture as better or more valuable than the cultures of others, and always avoid "*we—they*" language.
    *   Commit to the spirit of mission of the New Evangelization and its ongoing transformation of all cultures by gospel values.

3. Plan with the people, not for the people:
    *   First, listen to and welcome the unique perspectives of the diverse parishioners you are trying to reach.
    *   Include them—from the beginning—in the development of plans, programs, and activities.
    *   Avoid planning for others and judging them when they don't show up to your activity.

4. Broaden your understanding of ministry groups, programs, and structures, and cast a bigger net:
    *   Recognize the unique experiences, needs, and aspirations of each cultural/ethnic community in your parish.
    *   Understand that the existence of more than one cultural group in your parish is a blessing.

- Promote the formation of culturally specific groups and apostolic movements.
- Avoid the perception that allowing the formation of culturally specific groups creates division or separation.
- Commit to creating welcoming spaces for all Catholic people living in your parish.

5. Empower people from different cultures and ethnicities into leadership positions:
   - Understand the way in which people from different cultures view leadership, organize themselves, and make decisions.
   - Identify indigenous leaders and mentor them into leadership positions in ministry within their own cultural/ethnic community and in the parish as a whole.
   - Avoid a mentality of scarcity—"there is not enough for everyone"—and foster a vision of mission and growth that generates more resources and abundance for all.

RESOURCES

Brothers and Sisters to Us: United States Bishops' Pastoral Letter on Racism in Our Day. Washington, DC: USCCB, 1979.

CARA. "Parish Survey Project," in *The Changing Face of U.S. Catholic Parishes*. Washington, DC: Georgetown University, 2011. *www.cara.georgetown.edu*.

Pope John Paul II. *Ecclesia in America*. Washington, DC: USCCB, 2000.

Schreiter, Robert J., CPPS. *The Ministry of Reconciliation: Spirituality and Strategies*. Maryknoll, NY: Orbis Books, 1998.

Strangers No Longer: The Journey of Hope, A Pastoral Letter of the U.S. Bishops on Migration. Washington, DC: USCCB, 2003.

USCCB. *Asian and Pacific Presence: Harmony and Faith*. Washington, DC: USCCB, 2001.

USCCB. *Encuentro and Mission: A Renewed Pastoral Framework for Hispanic Ministry*. Washington, DC: USCCB, 2002.

USCCB. *Native American Catholics and the Millennium*. Washington, DC: USCCB, 2002.

USCCB. *Reconciled Through Christ: On Reconciliation and Greater Collaboration Between Hispanic American and African American Catholics*. Washington, DC: USCCB, 1997.

What We Have Seen and Heard: A Pastoral Letter of the African American Bishops on Evangelization. Washington, DC: USCCB, 1984.

GROUP ACTIVITIES

1. Using the nine movements in the process of ecclesial integration, reflect on where (what stage) your parish, diocese, school, or organization may be in the process. Share your reflections with others.

2. Read, reflect, and pray with John 21:1-17. Share your reflections regarding a spirituality of hospitality, reconciliation, and mission for ecclesial integration.

APPENDIX 1

Intercultural Communication: The Mutual Invitation Process

Respectful Communication Guideline

R: take **RESPONSIBILITY** for what you say and feel, and speak with words others can hear and understand

E: use **EMPATHETIC** listening, not just words but also feelings being expressed, non-verbal language including silence

S: be **SENSITIVE** to differences in communication styles

P: **PONDER** on what you hear and feel before you speak

E: **EXAMINE** your own assumptions and perceptions

C: keep **CONFIDENTIALITY**

T: **TRUST** the process because we are *not* here to debate who is right or wrong but to experience true dialogue

The Invitation Method is a way to include all people in the conversation in a very respectful atmosphere. While each person is speaking, the others listen. No one may interrupt the speaker or jump in to speak without being invited by name. In this method, no one has more authority than anyone else—each person is invited to share, and after sharing that person has the privilege to invite who will share next.

PURPOSE: To ensure that each person in the group is invited by name to share in an atmosphere of mutual respect.

METHOD:

1. The leader clarifies what the group members are being invited to share.
2. The leader gives guidelines about the use of time.
3. The leader may share first or may invite another person by name to share.
4. Who you invite does not need to be the person next to you.
5. After the person has spoken, that person is given the privilege to invite another to share.
6. If the person invited chooses not to share, the person may simply say "pass" and proceed to invite another to share.

    No explanation is needed or given for passing.
7. The process will continue until everyone has been invited to speak.
8. At that time, any person who passed will be invited again to share. Persons are still free to pass.
9. The main activity of the group is to listen.

—Eric H. F. Law, *The Wolf Shall Dwell with the Lamb*

Used by permission. All rights reserved. Kaleidoscope Institute. *www.kscopeinstitute.org.*

APPENDIX 2

Working with Groups in Intercultural Settings: A Cycle of Adaptation and Models of Multicultural Living

Many years ago, James Banks proposed that immigrants often go through a cycle of adaptation to their new culture. This cycle is helpful in understanding why immigrant communities will respond differently at different times. There are four stages in the cycle: immersion, withdrawal, negotiation, and institutionalization.

Immersion

In the first stage, immigrants eagerly try to adapt to the new culture, especially if they have come voluntarily to the new country. Eventually, however, they run into obstacles: the difficulty and complexity of the task, unforeseen challenges, or rejection by the prevailing culture. Any of these will dampen their initial enthusiasm.

Withdrawal

As a result of their loss of motivation for adapting to the new culture, immigrants will sometimes withdraw into their own culture, emphasizing their own language and customs over and against those of the prevailing culture. This is a time for regrouping and strengthening immigrants' self-esteem.

Negotiation

Newly strengthened by the withdrawal, immigrants will then re-enter the fray and try to negotiate with the prevailing culture to get some social space for aspects of their own culture, such as use of their own language, recognition of their customs and cultural artifacts, or celebration of their special feast days. By so doing, their competence face is acknowledged and recognized.

Institutionalization

The stage of institutionalization is reached when the prevailing culture comes to understand and accept the cultural contribution of an immigrant group as part of the prevailing culture. We have seen this especially in the United States as specific types of ethnic food (e.g., pizza, tacos) have come to be seen as simply "American food."

This cycle may repeat itself as immigrant cultures continue to find a place in the prevailing culture. This pattern may be particularly intense in the case of second-generation adolescents who may demand recognition of certain practices, but by the time they have been implemented by adults, the practices are no longer of interest to the adolescents.

Over the years of encounter between cultures, three models of living amid many cultures have developed. They might be designated as follows: *assimilation, multiculturalism,* and *selective adaptation.*

Assimilation

Assimilation assumes that the culture of immigrants will eventually dissolve and immigrants will gradually become indistinguishable from those of the prevailing culture. Language is usually the first aspect of immigrant culture to dissolve, followed by values and customs. Often, food is the only cultural component that remains.

The image here is of the "melting pot." (The term came from a 1905 Broadway play of the same name, written by a Russian immigrant named Israel Zangwill.)

The concept of a cultural "melting pot" was widely held in the United States until the 1970s. While it does describe what frequently (but not always) happens among immigrant groups, it failed to show respect for cultures. Assimilation is a view from the prevailing culture that does not take into account the experiences and feelings of immigrants about their own cultures.

Multiculturalism

This concept first appeared in the 1970s, and it was seen as a response to the weaknesses of assimilation. Multiculturalism stressed the right of people to maintain their distinctive cultures. Rather than a "melting pot," the image was one of a "salad bowl" in which the ingredients maintain their integrity while mutually contributing to the flavor of the whole.

The model of multiculturalism remained in favor until the late 1990s and is still used by many people today. However, it lost appeal in some circles for two reasons. First, it misreads what often happens to minority cultures in a new setting. It is difficult to maintain the complete integrity of a minority culture within a powerful prevailing culture, and there is some inevitable erosion. Thus, multiculturalism ignores the dynamics of power at work in such settings.

Second, a policy of maintaining cultures in their total integrity can lead to a lack of integration or engagement with the prevailing culture that adversely affects the economic and even social well-being of a minority culture. This is not as evident in the United States as it is in many European countries, where a *laissez-faire* mentality and a rather generous welfare system allow immigrants to remain disengaged from the larger culture, even into the third generation.

Occasionally, emerging leaders from particular groups are deprived of their own time and place to develop. Special development opportunities can occur in the name of multiculturalism, but they may be eliminated for economic reasons when departments are downsized and programs are merged. Sometimes this is inevitable, but the possible diminishment of emerging cultural groups and leaders needs to be considered and, if possible, avoided.

Selective Adaptation

A new model is arising in response to the weaknesses of the concept of multiculturalism. It does not yet have an accepted name, but it might be called "selective adaptation." This model tries to balance the need for cultural integrity and respect of immigrant cultures with the inevitable loss of elements in those cultures to the prevailing culture and the economic and social necessity of engagement with the prevailing culture. The precise method of creating the balance still needs to be resolved and may vary from community to community.

What should be enacted as a general social policy and what the Church should try to do in its ministry do not always exactly coincide. Because ministry is directed to the whole human person, it takes into account more than economic necessities. At the same time, culture should not be treated as a museum piece or an object of nostalgia.

APPENDIX 3

Developing Intercultural Sensitivity

This presentation aims at helping people track the growth of intercultural sensitivity in their pastoral settings. It largely follows the model developed by Milton Bennett in his essay titled "Toward Ethnorelativism: A Developmental Model of Intercultural Sensibility." His model proposes a progressing growth in intercultural sensitivity from high levels of prejudice to healthy interaction.

People unaware or unconnected to other cultures around them are often *ethnocentric*—that is, centered on their own culture as the only valid way to live in the world. To live any other way is deviant or substandard. This is an attitude found among those who are part of a prevailing culture that can afford to ignore other cultures around them. People growing up in a minority culture, on the other hand, are keenly aware of powerful "others" and learn from childhood how to survive in such situations. However, ethnocentrism can also be found among minority cultures and groups.

Bennett's model is intended especially for prevailing-culture individuals wanting to overcome ethnocentrism and develop greater intercultural sensitivity. It is especially useful in ministry settings for working with people who are part of the prevailing culture of the parish or school and feel they are being "invaded" by others. In addition, it can be helpful for all ministry staff members who are trying to understand such reactions and help move people along to greater empathy for others.

Bennett charts six stages on the path from ethnocentrism to what he calls "ethnorelativism." (Note: "Ethnorelativism" is probably not the best word to use

in ministry settings because "relativism" connotes indifference. A good substitute would be "healthy interaction" or even "communion.") Bennett's six stages to developing intercultural sensitivity are denial, defense, minimization, acceptance, adaptation, and integration.

Stage 1: Denial

Denial is a refusal to deal with the issue. It can be dealt with by trying to *isolate* the other culture away from ourselves (by not talking about it) or to *contain* it by seemingly benign stereotypes (such as treating the others as helpless children who cannot be mixed with the "adults").

Sometimes denial takes the form of maintaining a strict separation between ourselves and the other group. An example of this was the practice of setting up "chapels" for African Americans in white parishes.

Stage 2: Defense

When the "others" cannot be kept at arm's length any longer, a defensive attitude may set in. Because this attitude sees the other group as threatening, we have to take steps to defend ourselves. We then demonize members of the other group (see above) or denigrate them by using negative stereotypes.

At the same time, as we demonize or denigrate, we emphasize our own superiority.

Stage 3: Minimization

This is an attempt to minimalize the difference between ourselves and the "others." While such minimization may be well-intended and less adversarial than the first two stages, it is still a tactic to avoid engagement with the "others." Sometimes it does this by trivializing differences, acting as if the differences do not matter when in fact they do determine behavior. It may start from the assumption that culture is just an overlay on biology. Because all peoples share a common biology, the cultural differences are peripheral. Bennett calls this "physical universalism." At other times, a kind of "transcendent universalism" (Bennett's phrase) will be invoked. In church circles, as differences are being addressed, it is not uncommon to hear, "But we are all brothers and sisters in Christ!" This is indeed true, but in this particular setting, it is often a rhetorical stratagem to stop conversation about dealing with differences.

Stage 4: Acceptance

This marks the turning point in the process. In this stage, we move from defending ourselves from the "invading others" to finding ways of living and working together. At this point, difference begins to be valued more positively. We begin to realize that difference is irreducible and can even be helpful.

This step involves learning enough about others to come to respect their *behavioral differences* and realize that although their ways of acting and interacting are different, they have their own integrity. (The parameters presented in the second module of this workbook can be helpful here.) Also, behind those behavioral differences may be *value differences* that configure the world differently from our own. For example, what constitutes "family" is different in individualist and collectivist societies.

Stage 5: Adaptation

The next step after cognitively accepting difference is to take action. This involves adapting our own attitudes and behavior to accommodate the "others." Two adaptations are important here.

The first is *empathy*, or the capacity to feel what others feel and to see in some measure how they see the world. A capacity to experience empathy lays the groundwork for living and working together. Empathy is a little different from *sympathy*, which is the ability to show feelings of togetherness or solidarity toward others but always on our own terms.

The second is *pluralism*, or acknowledging that there are different and legitimate ways of living in the world. (In the context of a community of faith, this means recognizing that there are diverse and legitimate ways of living and even expressing such faith.)

Stage 6: Integration

At this stage, people become genuinely multicultural persons. We appropriate elements of the culture of the other group and make them our own, not in a patronizing, domineering, or colonizing way but by appreciating that their ways enrich our own culture or give better expression to our values. Their ways may address issues that our own culture does not do as well. Such integration makes interacting and appropriating *indispensable* for a fuller sense of life.

Bennett suggests that two outcomes are evident at this stage. The first is a capacity to evaluate behavior in light of its context, knowing that there is more than one perspective on the matter. He calls this "contextual evaluation."

The second demonstrates the capacity to stand outside a culture while having appropriate and effective interaction with it. He calls this "constructive marginality" because we are indeed in the margins of the culture, though we are not necessarily marginalized. We are able to engage the culture in appropriate and effective ways.

While reaching this sixth stage marks a certain completion of a journey from ethnocentrism to being able to work with other cultures well, it does not mark the end of learning about other cultures. This model shows the stages through which people go in becoming genuinely multicultural persons. As such, it provides a way of mapping a parish's or a community's capacity to interact with other cultures, and it can thus help ministers and staff move along to greater intercultural sensitivity.

Resources

Bennett, Milton. "Toward Ethnorelativism: A Developmental Model of Intercultural Sensibility." In *Education for the Intercultural Experience*, edited by R. Michael Page. Yarmouth, ME: Intercultural Press, 1993.

APPENDIX 4

Glossary of Terms

ACCULTURATION: The changes that take place as a result of continuous firsthand contact between individuals of different cultures; usually refers to the experiences of adults

ASSIMILATION: The process whereby an individual or group is absorbed into the social structures and cultural life of another person, group, or society

COMMUNICATION STYLE: A set of culturally learned characteristics associated with both language and learning style, involving such aspects of communication as formal versus informal, emotional versus subdued, direct versus indirect, objective versus subjective, and responses to guilt and accusation

CROSS-CULTURAL: The various forms of encounter and exchange between disparate cultural groups, often in a manner that reflects mutual respect

CULTURAL GENERALIZATION: The tendency to assume that a majority of people in a particular cultural group hold certain values and beliefs and engage in certain patterns of behavior. (A generalization is most appropriately based on research, held lightly as a hypothesis, and tested carefully by non-judgmentally observing the individual from another culture.)

CULTURAL STEREOTYPE: The application of a generalization to every person in a cultural group or generalizing from only a few people in a group. (Stereotypes are frequently based on limited experience, unreliable sources, hearsay, or media reporting. It is the rigid adherence to simplified perceptions of others, which is sometimes called "hardening of the categories.")

CULTURE: The learned and shared values, beliefs, and behaviors of a group of interacting people

CULTURE-SPECIFIC APPROACHES: Cross-cultural training approaches designed to prepare individuals to live and work with people of a particular culture or group

DEMOGRAPHICS: Vital statistics regarding age, gender, ethnicity, and so forth that characterize human populations. (Often generated from census data, demographics can be used to project future trends and to assist educators in meeting the needs of minority groups.)

DISCRIMINATION: A prejudiced or prejudicial outlook, action, or treatment (e.g., racial discrimination)

DIVERSITY (INCLUDING BOTH DOMESTIC AND GLOBAL DIVERSITY): Cultural differences in values, beliefs, and behaviors, including nationality, ethnicity, gender, age, physical characteristics, sexual orientation, economic status, education, profession, religion, organizational affiliation, and any other cultural differences learned and shared by a group of interacting people

ENCULTURATION: The sociological process of raising a child to be a member of a particular culture or cultural group (e.g., immigrant cultures adapting to the U.S.

experience). (Enculturation is not to be confused with inculturation, which is a theological and religious process.)

ETHNIC GROUP: Groups that share a common heritage and reflect identification with some collective or reference group, often in a common homeland. (Identification with an ethnic group is reflected in a sense of peoplehood, or the feeling that a person's own destiny is somehow linked with others who share this same ethnic background.)

ETHNIC IDENTITY: A sense of belonging and identification with one's ancestral ethnic group

ETHNOCENTRISM: The tendency that people have to evaluate others from their own cultural reference

EVANGELIZATION: Aimed at both the interior change of individuals and the external change of societies, the Church's evangelizing activity consists of several essential elements: proclaiming, preaching and bearing witness to Christ; teaching Christ; and celebrating Christ's sacraments. The four pillars or basic tasks of evangelization are (1) fostering a personal encounter with Christ; (2) inculturation or the transformation of cultures in light of Christian revelation; (3) liberation or the transformation of the social, economic, and political order by gospel values; and (4) ecumenical and interreligious dialogue in pursuit of unity among all peoples.

GENERALIZATION: An assumption that a majority of people in a particular cultural group tend to hold certain values and beliefs and engage in certain patterns of behavior. (This assumption can be supported by research and can be applied broadly to a large percentage of a given population or group.)

GLOBALIZATION: The process by which nations of the world become connected and interdependent through ties created by electronic communication, rapid means of travel, and interlocking economies

IMMIGRANTS: People who voluntarily move to a country of which they are not natives with the purpose of taking up permanent residence

INCARNATION: A central theological mystery and doctrine of Christianity that refers to the Second Person of the Blessed Trinity, the Son of God, becoming a human being in Jesus of Nazareth, a Galilean Jew, while also remaining God. St. John's Gospel refers to the Incarnation as the Word becoming flesh and dwelling among us (see Jn 1:15). This doctrine underlies the Catholic Church's identity and mission, which is to preach the Word of God and thus transform individuals, societies, and cultures in the image of Christ himself. This mystery also provides an example of unity in diversity to the extreme.

INCLUSION: The belief in and practice of creating heterogeneous groups and communities in classrooms, churches, and associations (e.g., the practice of teaching students with disabilities in regular classrooms); the opposite of exclusion. (Inclusion holds a certain affinity with the spirit of catholicity. At times, however, there may be quite legitimate reasons to exclude.)

INCULTURATION: A theological term for the engagement of Sacred Scripture and Church Tradition, especially the Gospel, in which culture is understood as a people's way of thinking, feeling, acting, and being; also called "evangelization of cultures." This process consists mainly of the transformation of a people's identity and deepest motivations and desires, especially their sacred stories, symbols, and rituals, through dialogue and the power of grace that accompanies the Christian proclamation. This process may pertain to discrete cultures (e.g., Mexican, United States, or Filipino) as well as to the overarching global cultures of modernity or postmodernity.

INDIGENOUS PEOPLE: People living in an area generally since prehistoric (or pre-European contact) times; related terms include aboriginal people (particularly in Australia) and first-nation people (particularly in Canada)

INTEGRATION: The process by which different groups or individuals are brought into a relationship characterized by mutuality and inclusiveness in such a manner as to create real unity in diversity without destroying the particularity and distinctiveness of each member

INTERCULTURAL COMMUNICATION: The study of theories and practices related to face-to-face interaction between people whose cultures are significantly different from one another

INTERCULTURAL COMPETENCE: A set of cognitive (mindset), affective (heartset), and behavioral (skillset) skills and characteristics that support effective and appropriate interaction in various cultural contexts

MARGINALIZATION: The practice of excluding a social group from the mainstream of the society, placing that group legally or socially on the "margins" of the society

MELTING POT: An image used to describe the process by which distinct cultures are totally assimilated into a new society and cease being what they were

MINORITY GROUP: A social group that occupies a subordinate position in a society, often experiences discrimination, and may be separated by physical or cultural traits that are disapproved of by the dominant group

MULTICULTURALISM: The re-elaboration of relationships within institutions or organizations as a result of the encounter of diverse cultures within them for the purpose of achieving integration rather than assimilation; a dynamic reality that occurs increasingly in the context of migration and the movement of people. (For the Catholic Church, multiculturalism has always been a fundamental feature of its catholicity and mission to preach the Gospel to all cultures and draw them into a communion in difference or diversity. Multiculturalism, however, has been critiqued for abetting a "one-size-fits-all mentality" in pastoral ministry by creating a situation in which all groups are put into the same basket. This can have a negative effect on diverse communities by depriving them of the exercise of subsidiarity and of opportunities to form their own leaders and develop appropriate pastoral and educational models, resources, and initiatives.)

NARRATIVE: A story that provides a cogent meaning for grasping and transcending one's reality by using imagination and insight to engage one's vision of the world and motivation for living; considered an element constitutive of cultures

NEW EVANGELIZATION: Re-proposing an encounter with Jesus Christ to people and cultures who have already been exposed to Christ and his message but have distanced themselves from them and participation in the life of the Church under the influence of secular society, particularly in Europe and North America. It also involves prayerfully listening to the contemporary world and proclaiming the Good News with renewed ardor, expressions, and methods that are mindful of the opportunities afforded by mass and social media as well as new technology.

PASTORAL DE CONJUNTO: Planned and collaborative pastoral activity that reflects a serious commitment to inclusivity, communion, and participation while paying attention to the ministerial and ecclesial reality and context. The concept for such activity originated in the thought of the episcopal conferences of Latin America, especially the documents of Medellín and Puebla. It was adopted in America through *Encuentro* processes and in documents such as the Catholic bishops of the United States' *National Pastoral Plan for Hispanic Ministry*.

PEOPLE OF COLOR: A phrase that refers to non-white minority group members, such as African Americans, Mexican Americans, Puerto Ricans, and Native Americans, but that also reflects recent demographic realities of the United States; often preferred over the phrase "ethnic minority" because these groups are, in many schools and communities, the majority rather than the minority

PREJUDICE: Uninformed judgments about others that are often unconscious, harsh, or discriminatory and that involve rejection

PREVAILING CULTURE: The culture of the social or political group that holds the most power and influence in a society; sometimes called the dominant culture

PROJECTION: The attribution of one's own ideas, feelings, or attitudes to other people or to objects, especially the externalization of blame, guilt, or responsibility as a defense against anxiety

RACE: In a biological sense, the clustering of inherited physical characteristics that favor adaptation to a particular ecological area. (Race is culturally defined in that different societies emphasize different sets of physical characteristics when referring to the concept of race. Thus, race is an important constructed, social characteristic not because of its biology but because of its cultural meaning in any given group or society.)

RACIAL IDENTITY: One's sense of belonging and identification with a racial group; may also refer to the categorization of an individual in terms of a racial group by society or other social groups

RACIAL PROFILING: The practice of constructing a set of characteristics or behaviors based on race and then using that set of racially oriented characteristics to decide whether an individual might be guilty of some crime and therefore worthy of investigation or arrest

RACISM: A social dysfunction characterized by an inability to see others as brothers and sisters, members of the same human family, because of the color of their skin or some other physical characteristic. (Significantly, racism is a social construct with no foundation in biology or any other science because the human family is so mixed genetically that there are no "pure" races.)

RITUAL: A repeatable, often customary action with deep meaning and significance by which persons express and reinforce relationships among themselves or with God; considered a constitutive element of culture

SHARED PARISH: A parish in which distinctive language or cultural groups share a common parish plant. (The term stands in contrast to "multicultural parish," which may raise ideological expectations or reflect a certain understanding as to how the diverse groups there interact or are supposed to interact. The term "shared parish" is neutral and raises fewer expectations.)

SECULARISM: A way of thinking, an ideology, that tends to ignore or reject values and concerns that spring from religious faith. It is a tendency to remove religious matters of ultimate concern from any consideration in the public square and relegate them to the private sphere. Religions thus lose social relevance.

SECULARIZATION: A social process whereby personal and institutional religious values and concerns are progressively relegated to the private sphere leading to a decline in the influence of faith and religious values on society in the public square

SOCIAL CLASS: The categorization of individuals in a stratified social system based on characteristics that are often related to (but may not be limited to) child-rearing practices, beliefs, values, economic status, prestige and influence, and general life chances

STEREOTYPES: Unsubstantiated beliefs about the personal attributes of the members of a group based on inaccurate generalizations that are used to describe all members of the group and that thus ignore individual differences

SYMBOL: A constitutive element of culture that Gerald A. Arbuckle defines as "emotionally experienced meaning" (*Culture, Inculturation, and Theologians*, Collegeville, MN: Liturgical Press, 2010)—that is, a sign expressing some reality in a graphic, emotionally moving, and motivating way (e.g., the U.S. flag, the Cross of Christ, the image of Our Lady of Guadalupe, or the Statue of Liberty)

THEOLOGICAL ANTHROPOLOGY: The relationship between human beings and God; the study of the meaning of human beings created in God's image and thus enjoying a special relationship with the divine as well as among themselves insofar as all mankind has but one common Creator, Redeemer, and Liberator: Jesus Christ

WHITE PRIVILEGE: The tendency of societies to conceptualize matters pertaining to race in terms of the perceptions and interests of the prevailing or dominant community (in the United States, of whites). White privilege is different from prejudice or racism in that it merely gives a special place, or privilege, to the concerns of one group. The features and causes of negative social, economic, or political circumstances faced by non-white people in U.S. society are largely ignored or denied. White privilege is a factor in creating what may be called society's tendency toward "benign neglect." However, this tendency is not exclusive to whites. Any group, if it attains a sustained level of hegemony, may fall prey to this tendency. For instance, in Mexico, which is a largely mestizo (mixed indigenous and Spanish heritage) nation, one might speak of a "mestizo privilege" that overlooks the realities faced by the indigenous or black people of Mexico.

APPENDIX 5

Sample Prayers and Liturgical Aids

Introduction

Building Intercultural Competence for Ministers was designed to begin and end with prayer. The prayers were composed to include the six cultural and racial families: Native Americans; African Americans; Hispanics; Europeans; Asian Pacific Islanders; and migrants, refugees, and travelers. These prayers include thanksgiving, petition, Scripture reading, reflection, and praise.

Opening Prayers

Activities

Offering of Symbols of Hope and Suffering

- In a meditative spirit, the witnesses from the different families, chosen two to three weeks before the training, are called upon to share their hopes and sufferings by bringing forward the different symbols that represent the hope and suffering of their respective cultural and ethnic communities in their daily lives.

- The witnesses offer the symbols at the altar as gifts that the families bring to the community of faith.

- They offer prayers to God so that through his Word, the people may be nourished and bear fruit.

- They offer prayers so that the community may remain hopeful in truth, justice, mutual love, and respect for one another.

Closing Prayer/Sending Forth Prayer

The purpose of the closing prayer is to lift the participants to God, asking God to bless them and their work. Each of the participants is prayed over and presented with a lighted candle. Inspired by the Holy Spirit, they are commissioned to carry the Gospel of peace and love to all peoples of all nations and cultures. "Go, therefore, and make disciples of all nations" (Mt 28:19). They must go forth to be leaven to themselves and others wishing to grow in unity and to become interculturally competent ministers.

Suggested Materials/Holy Objects

- Holy water
- Lighted candles
- Cross
- Holy Bible

Examples of Symbols of Hope and Suffering

Hispanic

Symbol of Hope: *Our Lady of Guadalupe*

Our Lady of Guadalupe is significant to Hispanic culture because it sends a message that the world of the indigenous people of the Americas is not over. This message is conveyed by the words of Our Lady and by her appearance as a young Native American woman. It sends a message that they are also children of the true God and that they will be taken care of. Further, Our Lady of Guadalupe chose Juan Diego, a Native American, to request that a temple be built on her behalf on the hill of Tepeyac so that the indigenous people could be heard, be consoled, and made to feel at home in the Church. With this symbol and shrine came the first massive evangelization movement of the Americas and a message of liberation, harmony, and hope that is still important to Hispanic Catholics today.

Symbol of Suffering: *Cristo Mojado*

This image, the Wet-Back Christ, is significant to Hispanic culture because it represents the difficult journey that thousands of Hispanics and other undocumented immigrants endure when attempting to enter the United States every year. This image calls us to be mindful of the hundreds of people who die each year trying to cross the border between the United States and Mexico. The image is born of a belief that people of the faith have to respond to the plight of our brothers and sisters who are coming to our country to work and yet are often treated like criminals.

African American

Symbol of Hope: *Daniel Rudd's picture*

Daniel Rudd has become a symbol of hope for African American Catholics. He was a passionate advocate for the Catholic Church, becoming an advocate for justice and freedom for African Americans. He gave voice to this cause through the development of the National Black Catholic Congress. There were five Congresses in the 1800s, and there have been five more Congresses since. The XI Congress will be held in the summer of 2012.

Symbol of Suffering: *Chains or slave ship; a book of slave narratives*

It has been almost 150 years since Abraham Lincoln issued the Emancipation Proclamation on January 1, 1863, yet racism is still a challenge. Specific concerns are poverty, housing, health care, prison systems, inclusion, and inclusive ministry.

European American

Symbol of Hope: *Celtic Cross*

Irish Catholics believe that the Celtic Cross became an emblem of the Celtic Christian Church when the Celts converted from paganism to Christianity. They believe that the circle on the cross is a symbol of eternity that emphasizes the endlessness of God's love. The appearance of the circle has also been explained by the Irish Catholics as the mystery of the Crucifixion and Resurrection of Christ.

Symbol of Suffering: *Letters*

The letters represent the prejudice that was expressed against Irish immigrants simply in response to the spelling of their last names. One Irish immigrant reportedly could not find a job after a period of rejection. Finally, someone made the comment to him that if he learned to spell his name "right," he might find a job. He accordingly changed the spelling of his name to reflect a Scottish spelling rather than an Irish one, and he found a job shortly after.

Asian and Pacific Islander

Symbol of Hope: *Bamboo plant*

For several Asian cultures, the bamboo plant, which has a long life, symbolizes longevity. Bamboo also has positive spiritual significance. There are many merits of bamboo according to its characteristics. Its deep roots denote resoluteness, and its straight, long stems represent pliability and adaptability when strong winds blow. The latter attribute plays a positive role in encouraging people to hold on when facing tough situations.

Symbol of Suffering: *Internment camps for Japanese Americans*

The internment camps for Japanese Americans during World War II and the "yellow peril" discrimination against the Chinese and other Asians are symbols of social actions and attitudes that do not permit full integration. Such actions and attitudes fail to recognize the many contributions of Asian and Pacific Islanders to American society and to the Church.

Native American

Symbol of Hope: **Blessed Kateri Tekakwitha**

Blessed Kateri Tekakwitha, who will soon be St. Kateri Tekakwitha, is a symbol of hope for Native American Catholics because she is the first and only Native American in the United States and Canada to be beatified by the Roman Catholic Church. She is a hero and role model for all Roman Catholics because she lived a life of great sanctity. She also exhibited great courage in the face of the extreme opposition and persecution that she experienced as she boldly strove to follow our Lord, Jesus.

Symbol of Suffering: **Faceless Native American infant doll**

The faceless Native American infant doll calls to mind the unjust activities of the U.S. government and other institutions to assimilate North American Indians into the mainstream through the various efforts they undertook to wipe out their identities and cultures. One of the most heinous and devastating programs was the removal of Native American children from their families and communities and forced placement in residential boarding schools. This was done with total disregard for their basic, God-given dignity and freedom.

Migrant, Refugee, and Traveler

Symbol of Hope: **SKU (Unity Symbol)**

The *unities* are treasured throughout Africa as a symbol of the African struggle for freedom and as a symbol of family and the unity of the people. Each of the *unities* teaches simple lessons of love, life, and harmony. Each of the *unities* shows the harmony of people within a community.

Symbol of Suffering: **Ship**

Amidst the strong wind and waves that batter the ship, which symbolize our earthly journey, Christ—our Way and our Light—leads us safely toward the eternal homeland.

Sample Opening Prayer/Liturgy

CALL TO PRAYER

Leader: Gathered together this evening and knowing that You, Lord, who show no partiality, are in our midst, we pray that we may be mindful that it is through You alone that we have gathered in this space. Send forth Your Spirit to enlighten our minds and enable our hearts as we continue our service as ministers and leaders. Keep us diligent in our tasks and caring in our relationships, and provide us with the tools to effectively carry out our duties and responsibilities to all people of all cultures and backgrounds. This we ask through Jesus Christ, our Lord.

Amen.

Opening Song: *We Are Your People*

Offering of Symbols
    Offering of Symbols of Hope
    Offering of Symbols of Suffering

INVOCATION

Side 1: Let us begin in the name of the Father, and of the Son, and of the Holy Spirit. Amen.

Side 2: We gather to proclaim the greatness of our Lord,

Side 1: To acclaim the beauty of His creation,

Side 2: To listen to the voices and heartbeats from the distant lands.

Side 1: We praise You; we welcome You in our gathering,

Side 2: Father, Son, and Holy Spirit, Trinity in unity undivided.

Side 1: God of protection, God of unity, God who loves us and blesses us,

Side 2: God who cares for His suffering people,

Side 1: We thank You for the wonder of our being.

Side 2: May all our activities for this special event nurture our faithfulness to your divine calling.

Side 1: May it promote peace, love, unity, and justice among Your children.

Side 2: God, plant the seed of true wisdom in our hearts; may we love and respect others as you do.

All: Word of comfort, come heal us, come fill our hearts, come renew us, and bring us hope.

Scripture Reading: Acts 10:34-43

Then Peter proceeded to speak and said, "In truth, I see that God shows no partiality. Rather, in every nation whoever fears him and acts uprightly is acceptable to him. You know the word (that) he sent to the Israelites as he proclaimed peace through Jesus Christ, who is Lord of all, what has happened all over Judea, beginning in Galilee after the baptism that John preached, how God anointed Jesus of Nazareth with the holy Spirit and power. He went about doing good and healing all those oppressed by the devil, for God was with him. We are witnesses of all that he did both in the country of the Jews and (in) Jerusalem. They put him to death by hanging him on a tree. This man God raised (on) the third day and granted that he be visible, not to all the people, but to us, the witnesses chosen by God in advance, who ate and drank with him after he rose from the dead. He commissioned us to preach to the people and testify that he is the one appointed by God as judge of the living and the dead. To him all the prophets bear witness, that everyone who believes in him will receive forgiveness of sins through his name."

The Word of the Lord.

R. Thanks be to God.

Reflection:

"The truth I have come to realize is that God has no favorites, but any person of any nationality who fears God and does what is right is acceptable to him."
Acts 10:34-35

As we gather to reflect on the significance of our ministry of building intercultural competence in the Church, we make the above expression of St. Peter our own. St. Peter was convinced of this truth in his outreach ministry to Cornelius and others who were outside the traditional Jewish culture. We must recognize that cultural diversity has changed the demographic reality of the Church in the United States.

When we celebrate our cultural diversity, we do not do it for the sake of promoting diversity, but in appreciation of this great gift of God to humanity, as manifested in our various cultural backgrounds.

This training is an opportunity for us to celebrate the richness of human culture. The richness of various cultures must be recognized, admired, and cherished. The Gospel proclaimed and lived by each person is distinct from but closely linked with the culture in which the person is rooted. As *Encuentro and Mission* states, "Ministry in the twenty-first century calls for a two-fold commitment to unity in diversity: to welcome and foster the specific cultural identity of each of the many faces in the Church, while building a profoundly Catholic identity that strengthens the unity of the one body of Christ."

This is our calling; this is our ministry for the Church and for people of all cultures.

PRAYER OF INTERCESSION

Response: Oyenos, Señor;
Ding gin mo ka mi;
Xin nham loi chung con;
Hear our prayer, O Lord.

1. Let us pray that people everywhere may recognize in various cultures the blessings of God to humanity. We pray to the Lord.
2. That people of different cultures may be inspired by the Spirit to use their gifts for the building of God's Kingdom on earth. We pray to the Lord.
3. That strangers and people from foreign cultures may find a place of welcome and love among us. We pray to the Lord.
4. That Christians everywhere may be encouraged and empowered to live out their faith within their cultures. We pray to the Lord.
5. That God may eradicate discrimination and cultural prejudice among Christians everywhere. We pray to the Lord.

CLOSING PRAYER

Eternal and loving God, You are the Creator of all that exists. You sent your Son into our world, born within a human culture. Open our eyes to your blessings in the world; inspire us to use them for your good and for the good of all. Help us to appreciate and encourage one another as members of your Holy Church and citizens of your Kingdom. Heal the wounds that separate us from one another and from your love, and bind us together as one family in Christ Jesus, Your Son. We ask this through our Lord, Jesus Christ, your Son, who lives and reigns with you and the Holy Spirit, one God for ever and ever.

Amen.

Sample Closing and Sending Forth Liturgy

INVITATION TO PRAYER

Let us begin in the name of the Father, and of the Son, and of the Holy Spirit. Amen.

OPENING SONG

OPENING PRAYER

Loving God, you give your gifts of grace for every time and season as you guide us in the marvelous ways of your love. Send your Spirit to open our minds and hearts to that love and show us how to live it in our different ministries. May God the Father, God the Son, and God the Holy Spirit fill each of us with faith, hope, and love. We ask this through your Son, Jesus. Amen.

PRAYER OF INTERCESSION

Side 1: Spirit of God, give us your gifts of wisdom and knowledge.
Side 2: Come, Holy Spirit.

Side 1: Spirit of God, give us your gifts of understanding and counsel.
Side 2: Come, Holy Spirit.

Side 1: Spirit of God, give us your gifts of fortitude and piety.
Side 2: Come, Holy Spirit.

Side 1: Spirit of God, give us your gift of holy fear of the Lord.
Side 2: Come, Holy Spirit.

BLESSING OF THE CANDLE AND PRESENTATION OF THE CANDLE AND CROSS

(Name), may God help you to be a light for others as Jesus calls us to be.

Response: Amen.

Song: *This Little Light of Mine*

Song: *We Are Marching in the Light of God/ Siyahamba*

CLOSING PRAYER AND BLESSING

O God, you have instructed the hearts of the faithful by the light of your Holy Spirit. Grant that by that same Spirit we may judge what is truly right and ever rejoice in your consolation. May we be constant reminders of the Spirit and of the blessings we have received. May we continue to live in a manner worthy of our calling, with humility and gentleness, with patience and respect, bearing with one another through love, striving to preserve the unity of the Spirit through the bond of peace. We ask this through Christ, our Lord. Amen.

NOTES